Title: ServiceNow AI Agent Playbook
Build, Train, Transform

Subtitle: The Go-To Playbook for ServiceNow Champions Delivering AI at Scale

By **Chirag Suthar**

Dedication

To my beloved parents—whose values, strength, and blessings have shaped every step of my journey.

To my wife—your unwavering support, patience, and belief in my vision gave this book its foundation.

To my siblings—thank you for being my constant source of inspiration and encouragement.

And to my bosses from my current and previous organisations —your mentorship, leadership, and trust have been instrumental in my professional growth and this publication.

To the visionaries and trailblazers who are driving digital transformation—this book is for you. May this playbook help you navigate the complex yet exciting journey of deploying AI in your enterprise.

This book is a reflection of the collective guidance, love, and empowerment you've all given me. I am forever grateful.

Table of Contents

CHAPTER 1:
INTRODUCTION

Welcome to the *ServiceNow AI Agent Factory Playbook: Build, Train, Transform*. This playbook is designed as the definitive guide for enterprise architects, platform owners, developers, and ServiceNow champions who are seeking to deliver enterprise-grade AI at scale. As organizations pivot toward hyperautomation, predictive operations, and autonomous service delivery, ServiceNow's AI Agent Factory becomes the cornerstone for intelligent transformation.

"AI is not just a technology—it's a transformation catalyst. The ServiceNow platform enables this transformation through AI Agents that learn, adapt, and scale." – John Ball, SVP & GM, ServiceNow Customer & Industry Workflows

This playbook will help you:

- Understand the end-to-end lifecycle of AI Agents on ServiceNow

- Define and build a scalable AI Agent Factory

- Leverage use cases and implementation blueprints across industries

- Apply people, process, and technology alignment strategies

- Measure outcomes with KPIs and transformation metrics

Whether you're starting with a Proof of Concept (PoC), scaling AI agents across business units, or creating a Center of Excellence (CoE) for AI, this guide will support your vision.

CHAPTER 2: THE EVOLUTION OF AI IN SERVICENOW

Artificial Intelligence in ServiceNow has evolved from rule-based automation to predictive intelligence and generative AI-powered agents. With each release—from New York to Washington DC—the capabilities have grown exponentially:

- **Early Phase**: Predictive Intelligence using machine learning models for ticket categorization and assignment.

- **Mid Evolution**: Virtual agents with predefined flows and NLP models.

- **Current State**: Generative AI, AI Search, Now Assist for ITSM, CSM, HRSD, SecOps, etc.

- **Future Vision**: Autonomous workflows, Agentic AI, and continuous self-learning agents.

Key enablers:

- Now Platform's **AI Framework**

- NLU/NLP with **Language Models**

- **Vector Search & Embeddings**

- **AI Data Lifecycle Management**

- **AI Agent Designer Studio** (Tokyo onwards)

"From scripted automation to self-learning agents, AI has become intrinsic to ServiceNow's value proposition."

CHAPTER 3: UNDERSTANDING THE AI AGENT FACTORY

The **AI Agent Factory** is a purpose-built methodology within the ServiceNow platform that accelerates the design, training, deployment, and scaling of AI-powered agents across the enterprise. Think of it as the AI equivalent of an agile DevOps pipeline—focused not on traditional code, but on intelligent behavior and continuous learning.

What is the AI Agent Factory?

The AI Agent Factory is both a framework and a suite of tools that enables organizations to:

- Design and prototype AI Agents with business logic and intent

- Train agents with curated enterprise data sets

- Deploy agents into production with monitoring and governance

- Iterate and continuously improve agent performance based on real-world interactions

Core Components

Component	Description
AI Agent Designer	Visual studio to create AI agent

	personas and behaviors
Training Pipelines	Configurable workflows for training LLMs or NLU models
Knowledge Orchestration	Ingest and optimize content from structured/unstructured sources
Embedded Governance	Versioning, ethical AI compliance, and traceability
Performance Dashboards	Monitor agent interactions, response quality, and user satisfaction

People, Process, Technology Alignment

People

- **AI Product Owners**: Define use cases and desired outcomes

- **Platform Architects**: Ensure scalable and secure design

- **Citizen Developers**: Empowered to build contextual agents

- **AI Trainers**: Curate and refine training data sets

Process

- Define use case and business value

- Create agent persona and knowledge boundaries

- Train and test agent with real scenarios

- Deploy and continuously monitor performance

Technology

- **ServiceNow Generative AI Controller**

- **AI Agent Designer** (from Washington DC release)

- **Document Intelligence, Virtual Agent, AI Search**

- **Integration with LLMs via Azure OpenAI, HuggingFace, etc.**

"The AI Agent Factory transforms AI from experimentation into scalable enterprise capability." – Dave Wright, Chief Innovation Officer, ServiceNow

CHAPTER 4: PAST, PRESENT, FUTURE OF AI ON SERVICENOW

Understanding the timeline and strategic vision behind AI on ServiceNow allows platform leaders to appreciate where AI has been, where it is now, and where it's heading. The maturity of ServiceNow AI reflects an intentional journey from operational automation to cognitive transformation.

Past: The Foundation of Predictive Automation

Before the AI boom, ServiceNow leveraged machine learning under Predictive Intelligence to classify, assign, and route tickets. Key milestones included:

- **New York to Quebec Releases**: Introduction of Predictive Intelligence and NLU capabilities

- **Virtual Agent Designer**: Drag-and-drop configuration of conversational flows

- **Training Pipelines for Ticket Categorization**: Based on historical data and Bayesian models

"Predictive Intelligence paved the way for more contextual and scalable automation in IT and employee workflows."

Present: Generative AI as a Strategic Enabler

With the arrival of GenAI capabilities, ServiceNow launched Now Assist and enhanced the Virtual Agent with large language model (LLM) integration:

- **Washington DC Release**: Full GenAI integration into ITSM, CSM, HRSD, SecOps

- **AI Search** and **Embedded Experiences** across portals and workspaces

- **ServiceNow Generative AI Controller** to plug in OpenAI, Azure OpenAI, and others

- **AI Agent Designer** with persona modeling and reusable behavior libraries

These capabilities allow:

- Dynamic summarization of incidents and knowledge

- Guided agent-assisted resolution and deflection

- AI-authored articles, responses, and diagnostics

Future: Toward Autonomous and Agentic Workflows

Looking ahead, ServiceNow aims to deliver autonomous agents that:

- Learn continuously through **reinforcement learning**

- Trigger and orchestrate **cross-platform actions** without human intervention

- Are embedded with **trust, ethics, and governance** models

- Operate in multi-agent environments (AI Agent Networks)

Key enablers on the roadmap include:

- **Custom LLMs trained on enterprise knowledge bases**

- **Federated learning** across business units and regions

- **Responsible AI Frameworks** for bias mitigation and transparency

- **Agent Interoperability Layer** (planned in Vancouver and beyond)

"The AI of the future on ServiceNow will not just respond, it will anticipate, decide, and act."

Absolutely. Let's now write a world-class Chapter 5 titled **"AI Agent Architecture and Taxonomy"**, integrating industry best practices, the ITIL framework alignment, KPIs, and the ServiceNow Platform's capabilities. This will be designed in a publishing-ready tone to contribute meaningfully toward the 130-page objective for Kindle distribution.

CHAPTER 5: AI AGENT ARCHITECTURE AND TAXONOMY

Designing AI Agents within the ServiceNow ecosystem demands a structured, modular architecture—one that not only aligns with platform capabilities but also with enterprise operational models, ITIL practices, and emerging AI governance frameworks.

"A well-architected AI Agent is not just built to serve tasks —it's built to evolve, govern, and scale." – Ludovic Blanchet, ServiceNow CTA Mentor

1. Architectural Layers of an AI Agent

An AI Agent in ServiceNow is structured through four primary architectural tiers:

1.1 Persona Layer (Who the agent is)

- Represents the *intent, context,* and *domain knowledge.*

- Modeled using the **AI Agent Designer Studio.**

- Includes tone, behavior style, scope boundaries, and escalation paths.

Example: A "Procurement Assistant" persona will only respond to Purchase Order-related queries, with boundaries clearly defined through intents.

1.2 Cognitive Layer (How the agent thinks)

- Leverages ServiceNow's **GenAI Controller**, LLMs, and **AI Search.**

- Supports intent classification, summarization, question answering, and document analysis.

- Applies **curated vector embeddings** using organizational corpus.

Tools & Components:

- Now Assist

- Document Intelligence

- Vector Database + NLP/NLU Pipelines

1.3 Process Execution Layer (What the agent can do)

- Connects the cognitive layer to the Now Platform's **workflow engine.**

- Executes tasks via **Flow Designer, Subflows, Script Actions,** or **Decision Tables.**

- Ensures tasks are ITIL-aligned (Incident, Request, Change, Problem).

Example: A Virtual HR Assistant can submit a Leave of Absence request and trigger the approval workflow, leveraging HRSD Catalog and Lifecycle Events.

1.4 Governance & Observability Layer

- Governs model versioning, ethical guidelines, and explainability.

- Integrated with **Performance Analytics**, **Agent Feedback Loops**, and **Compliance Audits**.

"Governance is the foundation. Without transparency and monitoring, AI turns from an asset into a liability." – KPMG AI Governance Lead

2. AI Agent Taxonomy

Taxonomy provides a classification schema to categorize AI Agents. It is essential to manage complexity and reusability across the enterprise.

Category	Description	Sample Use Cases
Task Agents	Execute discrete tasks	Reset password, Create PO, Open Incident
Knowledge Agents	Answer based on indexed content	Policy Q&A, Troubleshooting steps
Workflow Agents	Orchestrate cross-functional processes	Onboarding, Change Request
Advisory Agents	Provide recommendations	Incident RCA, SLA Breach Prediction
Autonomous Agents	Learn and act without prompts	Predict outages, Trigger patch cycles

3. Alignment with ITIL Framework

ServiceNow AI Agents must align with the ITIL Service Value System (SVS) and key practices:

- **Incident Management**: Auto-triage, classify, resolve, or escalate incidents.

- **Request Fulfillment**: Virtual Agent handling standard service requests.

- **Change Enablement**: Assist in change risk prediction and CAB preparation.

- **Knowledge Management**: Generate, validate, and

retire articles via AI-assisted authorship.

- **Continual Improvement**: AI-driven insights on SLA violations, root causes, and improvement plans.

4. Sample KPIs to Measure AI Agent Success

KPI	Description	Target
AI Resolution Rate	% of issues resolved without human intervention	> 60%
First Contact Resolution (FCR)	Resolutions provided on first interaction	> 70%
Agent Containment Rate	Interactions not escalated to humans	> 75%
Knowledge Usage Accuracy	Precision of content used by AI	> 85%
User Satisfaction (CSAT)	AI agent satisfaction score	> 4.3/5
Governance Compliance	Adherence to bias and explainability thresholds	100%

5. Best Practices for Designing AI Agent Architecture

- **Design for Modularity**: Use persona and intent modules that can be reused across agents.

- **Establish Guardrails Early**: Define escalation thresholds and response boundaries.

- **Data-Centric Training**: Train on curated, unbiased, and approved enterprise data.

- **Observe and Adapt**: Continuously monitor interaction quality and retrain.

- **Govern Like Code**: Treat AI models and personas as version-controlled digital assets.

"You don't deploy an AI Agent. You raise it—govern it, train it, measure it, and let it evolve." – CTA Panelist

---

CHAPTER 6: CREATING YOUR FIRST AI AGENT

Building your first AI Agent on the ServiceNow platform is a foundational milestone in operationalizing intelligent automation at scale. The process follows a structured lifecycle —from defining business value to training and deploying a responsive and governed AI persona.

"Success with AI starts not with code, but with clarity— clear intent, clear scope, and clear value." – KPMG Digital Transformation Director

---

⬚ Step-by-Step Guide to Building Your First AI Agent

1. Define Business Objective & Use Case

- Focus on high-value, high-volume use cases aligned with ITIL value chains.

- Collaborate with business and platform owners to define measurable outcomes.

Examples:

- Auto-triage and classify IT incidents

- Answer HR policy queries

- Summarize customer complaints

"Start with a use case where ROI can be clearly measured in time saved, satisfaction increased, or tickets deflected." – John Ball, SVP, ServiceNow

2. Create the Agent Persona Using AI Agent Designer

- Navigate to: **AI Agent Designer > Create New Agent**
- Define:
    - Agent name and intent (e.g., Procurement Assistant)
    - Domain knowledge and operational scope
    - Tone, escalation rules, behavior model

Best Practice: Use prebuilt templates for ITSM, HR, or CSM agents where available.

3. Define Knowledge Boundaries and Intent Scope

- Connect to specific KB articles, FAQs, or document repositories.
- Use **intent classification models** with ServiceNow's NLP capabilities.

"The more precise your scope, the more trustworthy your agent." – Ludovic Blanchet, CTA Coach

4. Train the Agent with Enterprise Data

- Go to: **AI Training Pipelines**
- Select:
    - Source documents (cleaned and approved)
    - Embedding strategy (vector indexing for semantic search)
    - Intents and utterances for training context

Best Practice: Use human-in-the-loop curation to improve accuracy before production.

5. Configure Generative AI with LLMs

- Navigate to: **Generative AI Controller**

- Configure:
  - LLM provider (OpenAI, Azure OpenAI, private models)

  - Prompt orchestration and context chaining

  - Ethical guidelines and model restrictions

Tip: Always test prompt behavior with real-world queries.

6. Orchestrate Agent Tasks with Workflow Integration

- Map intents to backend actions via:
  - Flow Designer

  - Script Includes

  - REST Integrations

Example:

- "Reset password" → Trigger Reset AD Credentials subflow automatically

"An agent is intelligent not only in conversation, but in action." – Marc Herni

7. Embed Governance and Feedback Controls

- Set escalation paths and audit mechanisms.

- Monitor:
  - Misclassification rates

- Bias detection
- Feedback scores

Governance Tools:

- Performance Analytics
- Model Version Control
- Feedback Tagging

8. Test the Agent in Lower Environment

- Use Test Agent in AI Agent Designer:
  - Simulate ambiguous queries
  - Validate knowledge boundaries
  - Confirm escalation triggers

Best Practice: Conduct business-user testing and include negative testing scenarios.

9. Publish to Production and Monitor Performance

- Use Agent Lifecycle Management to deploy agent.
- Track KPIs with embedded dashboards.

Sample KPIs for Post-Go-Live Monitoring

KPI	Description	Target
AI Resolution Rate	% of interactions resolved by agent	> 60%
Containment Rate	% of conversations not requiring human takeover	> 75%
User Satisfaction (CSAT)	Feedback score from end users	> 4.3 / 5

First Response Time	Time to first answer by AI	< 2 seconds
Escalation Accuracy	Correctness of hand-off to human agent	> 90%
Governance Compliance	Adherence to AI ethics & transparency	100%

Final Tips

- **Start Small, Scale Fast**: Begin with one or two agents and evolve into a factory model.

- **Empower Your Team**: Train AI Champions and platform admins to use AI Agent Designer.

- **Measure Everything**: Establish clear KPIs from the start and build feedback loops.

"You don't just build an AI Agent—you cultivate it. Train it, monitor it, refine it, and let it grow." – Dave Wright, Chief Innovation Officer, ServiceNow

CHAPTER 7:
STRATEGY &
ROADMAP FOR AI
AGENT ADOPTION

"AI transformation is not a project—it's a platform shift. Success depends on strategic alignment, not just technical execution."
— CIO, Fortune 100 Financial Institution

⬚ 1. Define Your North Star Vision

Every successful AI adoption begins with a bold but clear strategic intent. Define your **North Star** by aligning AI agent initiatives to the enterprise's digital transformation goals.

Key Considerations:

- Align with the organization's **ITIL service value chain**

- Integrate into **digital transformation OKRs**

- Map to measurable business outcomes (efficiency, cost reduction, satisfaction)

Vision Example: "By 2026, 70% of Tier 1 support interactions will be resolved autonomously through AI Agents with 4.5+ CSAT."

☐ 2. Build an AI Agent Adoption Roadmap

A well-structured roadmap bridges vision and execution. Design it in **three stages**:

Phase	Focus Area	Time Horizon	Examples
Phase 1: Foundation	Establish AI Agent Factory, PoC use cases	0–6 months	ITSM Agent, HR Policy Q&A
Phase 2: Expansion	Scale to other business units & workflows	6–18 months	CSM Assist, Procurement Bot
Phase 3: Transformation	Enable autonomous agents, CoE, federated learning	18–36 months	Predictive Ops, GenAI Dev Assistants

☐ 3. Define the AI Operating Model

Adopt a **federated model** that balances central governance with local innovation.

Roles & Responsibilities:

Role	Responsibility
AI Product Owner	Owns use case value, KPIs, backlog
Platform Architect	Designs scalable agent infrastructure
Agent Trainer	Curates and maintains training data
Business Process Owner	Validates outcomes and continuous feedback
AI Governance Lead	Ensures compliance, fairness, and transparency

☐ 4. Prioritize Use Cases with Impact Framework

Evaluate use cases using the **Value x Feasibility Matrix**:

- **Value**: Cost savings, FTE reduction, CSAT uplift, cycle time

- **Feasibility**: Data availability, LLM readiness, integration complexity

Tip: Start with high-frequency, well-documented, rule-based tasks—ideal for early wins.

---

5. Establish Governance & Trust Framework

Use a **Responsible AI Framework** tailored for the Now Platform:

- Data provenance and access control

- Audit trails for AI decisions

- Bias detection models

- Explainability and ethical escalation

- Retraining policies and agent version control

"Without trust, your AI agents will never be used—no matter how well they're built."
— ServiceNow Risk & Compliance Architect

---

6. Monitor and Optimize AI Agent Performance

Create dashboards using **Performance Analytics** and **Continuous Feedback** loops.

Sample Metrics:

- Resolution rate by agent

- Containment rate

- Agent learning curve slope

- SLA impact on service desk load

- CSAT trends post-deployment

Best Practice: Use A/B testing across AI agent versions to compare performance.

7. Scale with Center of Excellence (CoE)

Create an **AI Agent CoE** to standardize reusable components, share learnings, and enable democratized development via citizen developers.

Core Functions:

- Maintain best practice libraries

- Drive cross-BU AI agent reuse

- Define platform guardrails

- Run AI maturity assessments

8. Enable Change Management & Training

Successful adoption requires **human alignment**—not just machine learning.

- Conduct stakeholder workshops and readiness assessments

- Launch training programs for fulfillers and developers

- Publish AI agent FAQs, Do's & Don'ts, and escalation maps

- Communicate value to users and leadership through outcomes

"AI adoption succeeds not through technical wins—but through user belief in the outcomes."
– VP, Digital Experience Transformation, Global Manufacturing

Firm

Perfect. Let's continue with:

CHAPTER 8: BUILDING AN AI AGENT FACTORY STRATEGY

"You don't scale AI by building agents. You scale by building a factory that builds agents—securely, repeatedly, and intelligently."
—ServiceNow CTA Mentor

1. What Is the AI Agent Factory?

The **AI Agent Factory** is not a tool—it's a strategic operating framework that enables continuous, scalable, and governed development of AI agents on the Now Platform. Think of it as an *assembly line*—transforming data, workflows, and personas into intelligent agents that evolve over time.

2. Core Pillars of the AI Agent Factory

Pillar	Description	Key Capabilities
Design Studio	Visual creation of agents, intents, behaviors	Persona modeling, tone setup, scope mapping
Training Engine	Curate, embed, and test knowledge sets	Vector embedding, LLM configuration, real-user simulation
Deployment Pipeline	CI/CD for AI agents and updates	Agent staging, A/B testing, blue/green deployment
Monitoring Hub	Feedback, KPIs, user sentiment	CSAT, FCR, AI drift monitoring

Governance Layer	Risk, compliance, explainability	Audit trails, escalation guardrails, versioning policies

---

⬜ 3. Building the Factory on ServiceNow Platform

Step-by-step implementation guide:

1. **Enable AI Agent Designer Studio** (Washington DC release+)
   - Activate plugin: AI Agent Designer
   - Configure workspace access and permissions (sn_ai_agent.* roles)

2. **Integrate with Generative AI Controller**
   - Use connectors for Azure OpenAI, OpenAI, or HuggingFace
   - Map intents and behavior to appropriate LLM

3. **Set Up Vector Embedding Index**
   - Use **AI Search + Document Intelligence**
   - Index curated knowledge bases and historical resolutions

4. **Define Guardrails & Escalation Protocols**
   - Leverage Flow Designer + Decision Tables to define:
     - When to escalate
     - When to log and suppress
     - When to loop back for feedback

5. **Create Agent Training Pipelines**
   - Simulate user queries using predefined prompt libraries

- Use test harnesses to monitor performance thresholds

6. **Instrument Monitoring**
   - Enable **Performance Analytics** widgets for AI metrics
   - Capture user thumbs-up/down ratings, CSAT, and feedback

7. **Automate Retraining Loops**
   - Trigger retraining when:
     - CSAT drops below threshold
     - Accuracy rate falls by 10%
     - New domain knowledge is added

⬜ 4. Governance Blueprint

Adopt a governance strategy across three axes:

Axis	Governance Activity
Ethical	Bias testing, responsible content filters, LLM audit
Operational	Agent registry, SLA for response time, uptime monitoring
Security	Data privacy by design, access controls, escalation security patterns

"Governance doesn't slow you down. It gives you the license to scale with confidence."
— Chief Digital Risk Officer, Energy Sector

⬜ 5. Organizational Model to Support Factory

Structure your AI Agent Factory with the right talent and accountability model:

Role	Function
AI Product Manager	Owns use case pipeline, value realization
AI Architect	Defines design patterns, scalability frameworks
Trainer/Annotator	Manages training sets and prompts
Platform Owner	Ensures compliance, licensing, system performance
Fulfillment SMEs	Provide domain context, validate outputs

6. KPIs to Track Factory Maturity

KPI	Description	Maturity Target
# of AI Agents in Prod	Indicator of scale	20+ within 12 months
Agent Reusability Index	% of shared intents or personas	> 40%
Avg. Time-to-Deploy	Build to live cycle duration	< 4 weeks
CSAT (AI vs Human)	Satisfaction parity	±5% gap
Training Drift %	% of agent knowledge that's outdated	< 10%
Governance Score	Coverage of controls implemented	> 95%

7. Continuous Improvement Cycle

Adopt a DevOps-style cycle tailored for AI Agents:

Discover → Design → Train → Test → Deploy → Monitor → Improve

- Use Feedback → Fine-tune → Retrain → Publish

- Celebrate high-performing agents; sunset or merge underperformers

⬜ Best Practices for Building the Factory

- **Design Reusability First**: Modularize intents, behaviors, and personas.

- **Automate Everything**: Testing, retraining, escalation logging, CSAT analysis.

- **Involve Business Early**: Get domain input during persona modeling and scope definition.

- **Embed Guardrails**: Never launch an agent without fallback and ethical protocols.

- **Invest in Training Data**: Quality data = Quality outcomes.

"An AI Agent Factory is not about speed—it's about scale, stability, and sustained learning."
— CTA Panelist

Let's move forward with **Chapter 9: Use Cases Across Industries**.

CHAPTER 9: USE CASES ACROSS INDUSTRIES

"AI is not a one-size-fits-all solution; it's about crafting personalized experiences based on specific industry needs."
— John Ball, SVP & GM, ServiceNow Customer & Industry Workflows

---

⬚ 1. Introduction to AI Use Cases Across Industries

ServiceNow's AI-powered agents are transforming industries by solving domain-specific problems, improving customer service, and automating repetitive tasks. With ServiceNow's flexibility, businesses can tailor AI solutions to meet the unique demands of various sectors, from healthcare to finance to retail.

This chapter explores several **real-world AI Agent use cases**, demonstrating how AI-powered automation can unlock value and drive efficiency across different sectors.

⬚ 2. Healthcare: Empowering Patient and Provider Interaction

Healthcare organizations are utilizing AI agents to streamline workflows, enhance patient engagement, and reduce operational burdens.

Use Case 1: Virtual Health Assistant for Patients

AI agents are deployed as virtual health assistants to:

- **Pre-screen patients**: AI agents help triage patient symptoms and gather medical history before connecting with a healthcare provider.

- **Schedule appointments**: Automate the appointment booking process, rescheduling, and reminders.

- **Provide care guidance**: Offer health advice and follow-up instructions post-visit or procedure.

Benefits:

- Improved patient satisfaction with quick response times

- Reduced burden on healthcare staff by automating routine inquiries

- More personalized patient engagement based on historical health data

KPIs:

- Patient Satisfaction Score (CSAT): 85%+

- First Contact Resolution (FCR): 80%

- Reduction in Appointment No-Shows: 20%

🔹 3. Financial Services: Enhancing Customer Service and Risk Management

In the financial services sector, AI agents are helping streamline customer interactions and improve risk management processes.

Use Case 2: AI Chatbot for Financial Queries

AI agents are deployed to:

- **Assist with account management**: Provide customers with instant access to account balances, recent transactions, and product offerings.

- **Offer financial advice**: AI-driven agents provide real-time advice based on customer transaction history and market trends.

- **Automate compliance checks**: Review transactions for compliance with regulations and ensure customers meet regulatory requirements.

Benefits:

- Reduced customer service response times

- Enhanced compliance through automated checks

- Personalized financial advice leading to increased customer satisfaction

KPIs:

- Agent Containment Rate: 75%

- Average Resolution Time: 1 minute per query

- Customer Satisfaction Score (CSAT): 90%

⬜ 4. Retail: Personalizing Customer Experience

Retailers are increasingly leveraging AI agents to offer personalized shopping experiences and optimize inventory management.

Use Case 3: AI-Powered Virtual Shopping Assistant

AI agents can be used to:

- **Guide customers through the shopping process**: Help customers find products based on their preferences, budget, or previous purchase history.

- **Provide product recommendations**: AI agents

recommend products using customer data and predictive models.

- **Manage stock levels**: Automatically reorder products based on sales trends and seasonal demand.

Benefits:

- Enhanced customer shopping experience with personalized assistance

- Increased sales through product recommendations

- Improved inventory accuracy and management

KPIs:

- Conversion Rate: 25% increase

- Customer Retention Rate: 40%+

- Inventory Turnover Ratio: 10% improvement

---

5. Manufacturing: Streamlining Operations and Maintenance

In manufacturing, AI agents can streamline operational processes, reduce downtime, and support predictive maintenance.

Use Case 4: Predictive Maintenance Assistant

AI agents help manufacturing facilities:

- **Monitor equipment health**: AI agents monitor real-time sensor data to detect anomalies in machinery and predict failures before they occur.

- **Schedule maintenance**: Automate maintenance schedules based on real-time data analysis.

- **Manage parts inventory**: Keep track of spare parts

and automatically reorder when levels run low.

Benefits:

- Reduced downtime through proactive maintenance

- Optimized parts inventory and lower operational costs

- Improved worker safety with early detection of machine malfunctions

KPIs:

- Downtime Reduction: 15% decrease

- Mean Time Between Failures (MTBF): 10% increase

- Spare Parts Stockouts: Reduced by 20%

⬜ 6. IT Operations: Enhancing Incident Management and Support

AI agents play a crucial role in IT operations, reducing response times and improving problem resolution for both end users and IT support teams.

Use Case 5: AI-Driven Incident Resolution and Support

AI agents in IT operations are deployed to:

- **Automatically categorize and assign incidents**: AI agents analyze incoming incident tickets, categorize them based on urgency, and assign them to the right team.

- **Provide self-service support**: Offer automated troubleshooting guidance for common IT issues, such as password resets, software installation problems, and network connectivity.

- **Monitor system health**: Proactively detect and resolve issues in real-time.

Benefits:

- Faster incident resolution times and reduced human error
- Lower ticket volume for IT staff through effective automation
- Improved end-user experience with more immediate solutions

KPIs:

- First Contact Resolution (FCR): 90%
- Incident Triage Time: Reduced by 50%
- Agent Containment Rate: 70%

▢ 7. Public Sector: Optimizing Service Delivery and Citizen Engagement

Governments and public sector organizations can use AI agents to improve citizen engagement and service delivery while enhancing operational efficiencies.

Use Case 6: AI Assistant for Citizen Services

Public sector organizations deploy AI agents to:

- **Automate document processing**: AI agents can handle applications, renewals, and claims by scanning and processing citizen-submitted documents.
- **Provide instant responses**: AI agents can answer common questions about public services, benefits, and policies.

- **Support case management**: Track citizen requests and provide real-time updates on the status of applications or cases.

Benefits:

- Improved efficiency in service delivery

- Enhanced citizen satisfaction with faster response times

- Reduced administrative burden on public sector employees

KPIs:

- Citizen Satisfaction Score: 80%+

- Application Processing Time: Reduced by 30%

- Response Time for FAQs: <2 minutes

⬜ 8. Hospitality: Improving Guest Experience and Operational Efficiency

The hospitality industry is using AI agents to streamline guest interactions and enhance customer experience.

Use Case 7: Virtual Concierge Assistant

AI agents are deployed in hospitality to:

- **Assist with booking and reservations**: AI agents help guests with making, modifying, and canceling hotel reservations.

- **Provide personalized recommendations**: AI-powered agents recommend nearby attractions, restaurants, and local services based on guest preferences.

- **Manage guest requests**: Automate guest requests

such as room service, housekeeping, and maintenance.

Benefits:

- Enhanced guest experience with immediate responses

- Improved operational efficiency through automation

- Increased guest loyalty through personalized service

KPIs:

- Guest Satisfaction Rate (GSR): 85%+

- Reservation Modification Rate: 20% improvement

- Average Response Time for Requests: <1 minute

9. Future of AI Use Cases Across Industries

The future of AI-powered agents across industries is marked by the continuous evolution of generative AI, autonomous workflows, and multi-agent collaborations. Emerging technologies such as **reinforcement learning, edge computing**, and **5G** will further accelerate the development and deployment of sophisticated AI agents that will transcend existing use cases, drive even greater automation, and enhance personalized service delivery at scale.

"AI is the backbone of Industry 4.0. Its evolution across industries is just beginning, with limitless possibilities ahead."
— Marc Herni, ServiceNow CTA Panelist

Great! Let's move forward with **Chapter 10: Transformational Impact of AI Agents**.

CHAPTER 10: TRANSFORMATIONAL IMPACT OF AI AGENTS

"AI is the bridge between today's digital platforms and tomorrow's autonomous enterprises. ServiceNow's AI agents are reshaping business landscapes, driving efficiency, and fostering innovation."
— Dave Wright, Chief Innovation Officer, ServiceNow

1. Introduction to the Transformational Impact

AI agents on the ServiceNow platform represent a powerful catalyst for transformation, driving real business value and enabling organizations to operate in a more intelligent, automated, and agile manner. The introduction of AI agents extends far beyond mere task automation; it is about reshaping how businesses operate, innovate, and scale.

In this chapter, we'll explore how AI agents are transforming organizations by enabling predictive and prescriptive analytics, improving customer and employee experiences, enhancing decision-making, and facilitating real-time, data-driven insights. As businesses continue to evolve and face new challenges, AI agents are positioned as pivotal players in enabling this transformation.

2. Driving Operational Efficiency

One of the most significant impacts of AI agents is their ability to drive **operational efficiency**. By automating repetitive tasks and improving workflows, organizations can reduce manual intervention, accelerate response times, and optimize resources. This not only leads to cost savings but also frees up employees to focus on high-value tasks.

Use Case: Automated Incident Management

Through AI-powered **incident management**, businesses are leveraging AI agents to automatically categorize, assign, and prioritize incidents based on urgency and business impact. The automation of this process reduces the need for human intervention in ticket triage, thereby speeding up resolution times and improving service reliability.

Key Impact:

- Faster response times

- Reduced human error

- Greater focus on high-priority incidents

- Improved service continuity

KPIs:

- **MTTR (Mean Time to Resolve)**: Reduced by 30%

- **First Contact Resolution (FCR)**: Increased by 20%

- **Incident Triage Accuracy**: 95%+

☐ 3. Enhanced Decision-Making Through Predictive Analytics

AI agents go beyond rule-based decision-making by leveraging **predictive analytics** to forecast potential outcomes based on historical data. This empowers organizations to make more informed decisions in real-time, anticipate issues, and take proactive measures.

Use Case: Predictive Maintenance in Manufacturing

In industries such as manufacturing, AI agents can predict equipment failure before it happens. By analyzing real-time data from IoT devices and historical performance metrics, AI agents can forecast the lifespan of components and schedule maintenance before failure occurs, thus avoiding costly downtime.

Key Impact:

- Reduced downtime and disruptions
- Increased equipment reliability
- More proactive resource planning

KPIs:

- **Downtime Reduction**: 25%
- **Maintenance Cost Savings**: 20%
- **Operational Efficiency**: Improved by 15%

---

4. Elevating Customer Experience

AI agents are revolutionizing the **customer experience (CX)** by providing instant, personalized, and consistent interactions across multiple channels. From customer service chatbots to AI-powered self-service portals, AI agents are enabling businesses to deliver a higher level of engagement with customers, enhancing satisfaction and loyalty.

Use Case: AI-Powered Virtual Customer Assistant

AI-powered **virtual customer assistants** are enabling organizations to provide 24/7 customer support, handling a wide range of inquiries from order status to troubleshooting. With natural language processing (NLP) capabilities, these assistants understand and respond in a conversational tone, improving the overall customer experience.

Key Impact:

- Instant support and resolution

- 24/7 availability

- Personalized customer interactions based on historical data

KPIs:

- **Customer Satisfaction (CSAT)**: 90%+

- **Agent Containment Rate**: 70%

- **Response Time for Queries**: Less than 2 minutes

---

5. Real-Time Insights for Better Business Decisions

AI agents provide businesses with real-time **data-driven insights**, enabling quicker decision-making. With the ability to analyze large datasets quickly, AI agents can surface key insights that might otherwise be missed by human analysts.

Use Case: Intelligent Analytics for Business Operations

AI agents integrated with **performance analytics** can provide executives and managers with actionable insights about business performance, trends, and areas of improvement. These insights help guide decisions on strategy, resource allocation, and process improvement.

Key Impact:

- Faster decision-making

- Data-driven strategies

- Better alignment with business objectives

KPIs:

- **Decision-Making Speed**: 50% faster decisions

- **Actionable Insights Delivery**: Increased by 30%

- **Operational Visibility**: Enhanced by 40%

---

6. Empowering Employees and Facilitating Employee Experience

AI agents are not only transforming customer-facing operations but are also having a profound impact on **employee experience**. By automating routine administrative tasks and providing instant access to knowledge and tools, AI agents help employees focus on higher-value activities, boosting morale and productivity.

Use Case: AI-Driven Employee Self-Service

In large organizations, AI agents can act as a **self-service HR assistant**, helping employees with tasks such as vacation requests, benefits queries, and payroll information. These agents empower employees to resolve their issues independently, reducing the workload for HR teams and improving employee satisfaction.

Key Impact:

- Improved employee productivity

- Enhanced employee satisfaction

- Reduction in HR workload

KPIs:

- **Employee Satisfaction (ESAT)**: 85%+

- **Self-Service Adoption Rate**: 75%

- **HR Staff Time Saved**: 30%

---

7. Enabling Continuous Improvement and Agility

AI agents enable **continuous improvement** by learning from interactions and adapting to changing conditions. With built-in feedback loops, AI agents can evolve over time, becoming more accurate and efficient in addressing the needs of the business.

Use Case: Continuous Improvement through AI Learning

As part of the AI lifecycle, ServiceNow AI agents can be continually trained and refined based on data from previous interactions. This ongoing training ensures that agents stay up to date with the latest business processes, customer demands, and technological advancements.

Key Impact:

- AI agents that evolve and improve over time

- Continuous alignment with business goals

- Increased agility in response to changing market conditions

KPIs:

- **Agent Learning Rate**: 20% improvement per quarter

- **Customer Feedback Integration**: 90% accuracy in predicting customer needs

- **Process Efficiency Gains**: 10% improvement per cycle

8. Achieving Greater Scalability and Cost Efficiency

One of the most powerful aspects of AI agents is their ability to scale without adding proportional costs. As demand for services increases, AI agents can handle an exponential volume of tasks without requiring additional resources, making them highly cost-effective.

Use Case: Scalable IT Service Management

In IT service management (ITSM), AI agents can scale to

handle an increasing number of incidents and requests without additional IT staff. This scalability is achieved by automating routine tasks and empowering agents to self-resolve common issues, allowing IT staff to focus on more complex problems.

Key Impact:

- Cost-effective service delivery

- Scalable operations with no proportional increase in costs

- Improved service quality at scale

KPIs:

- **Cost Per Resolution**: Reduced by 25%

- **Agent Utilization Rate**: 90%

- **Scalability of Operations**: 50% increase in agent capacity

9. Future Impact: Autonomous Enterprises

As AI technology continues to evolve, AI agents will play an even more pivotal role in the transformation of businesses. The future of AI agents includes fully **autonomous enterprises**, where AI-driven systems can make decisions, execute actions, and manage workflows with little to no human intervention.

Vision for the Future: Autonomous AI-Driven Businesses

The next frontier for AI agents includes:

- **Autonomous decision-making**: AI agents will independently make business decisions based on predefined parameters, evolving market conditions, and real-time data.

- **Cross-agent collaboration**: AI agents will collaborate with each other across departments, sharing data and insights in real time to optimize outcomes.

- **Self-optimizing workflows**: AI agents will continuously improve workflows, ensuring that business processes are always optimized for efficiency and cost-effectiveness.

Key Impact:

- Fully autonomous operations
- Self-optimizing systems
- Real-time decision-making and execution

KPIs:

- **Autonomy Index**: 80% of tasks autonomously executed
- **Operational Efficiency Gains**: 40%
- **Cost Savings**: 30% reduction in operational costs

Conclusion: The Transformational Power of AI Agents

AI agents on the ServiceNow platform are not just transforming the way businesses operate—they are fundamentally reshaping industries, improving customer and employee experiences, and enabling organizations to unlock new levels of efficiency, scalability, and innovation. By continuously evolving and integrating into the broader business ecosystem, AI agents are paving the way for the next generation of enterprise automation and transformation.

CHAPTER 11:
BEST PRACTICES
FOR AI AGENT
DEVELOPMENT

"Developing AI agents isn't just about writing code; it's about understanding the business problem, ensuring transparency, and continuously iterating to improve performance and outcomes."
— Lisa Kim, Head of AI Research, ServiceNow

1. Introduction to Best Practices for AI Agent Development

AI agents on the ServiceNow platform hold immense potential, but to unlock their full capabilities, developers must follow best practices throughout the entire lifecycle—from design to deployment and continuous optimization. This chapter outlines key best practices to ensure that AI agents are effective, scalable, and aligned with business objectives.

By implementing these practices, organizations can ensure that AI agents deliver real business value, reduce risk, and provide long-term sustainability.

2. Understand the Business Problem and Define Clear Objectives

The foundation of any successful AI agent development lies in **understanding the business problem** and aligning the AI agent's functionality with business goals. Before diving into development, it's crucial to:

- **Collaborate with stakeholders**: Engage with business leaders, process owners, and subject matter experts to clearly define the objectives.

- **Identify key use cases**: Choose high-impact processes or pain points where AI can drive the most value, such as incident management, change requests, or employee onboarding.

- **Set measurable goals**: Establish clear, quantifiable KPIs to measure the success of the AI agent, such as reducing resolution time or improving user satisfaction.

Best Practice: Conduct a detailed requirements gathering phase before starting development, ensuring alignment between technical capabilities and business needs.

3. Start Small and Focus on a Single Use Case

AI development can be complex, so it's essential to **start small** with a focused, high-value use case. This helps mitigate risks and allows for easier refinement before scaling.

Example: Start with a Virtual Assistant for IT Service Management

Begin by building a virtual assistant to help users raise and track IT service requests. This smaller scope allows you to test the AI's capabilities, gather user feedback, and iteratively improve the agent before expanding to other areas like HR or finance.

Best Practice: Prioritize the use case based on the business value it can deliver and ensure that AI agents are aligned with these goals.

4. Design with the End-User in Mind

The success of AI agents heavily depends on **user adoption** and experience. To ensure high engagement and usability, design with the end-user in mind. Focus on the following:

- **Personalization**: Leverage user data and AI capabilities to provide a personalized experience. For example, an AI agent can offer tailored recommendations based on an individual's history and preferences.

- **Natural Language Processing (NLP)**: If you're developing a conversational AI agent, ensure it understands natural language inputs and responds in a way that feels human, engaging, and empathetic.

- **Clear Communication**: Always communicate what the AI agent can do, set expectations on response times, and ensure transparency around any limitations or fallback scenarios.

Best Practice: Continuously test the AI agent with real users to validate its design, performance, and accuracy, gathering feedback to improve over time.

5. Build an Iterative Development Process

AI agent development is not a one-time effort. Instead, it requires an **iterative approach** to refine and optimize the agent. Adopting Agile methodologies can help speed up development while ensuring continuous improvement.

- **Prototype quickly**: Start with a prototype that addresses the core functionality, then refine based on feedback.

- **Monitor performance**: Track the performance of AI agents regularly to assess accuracy, efficiency, and user satisfaction. This includes reviewing metrics like first-contact resolution rates and response times.

- **Plan for continuous learning**: Implement a feedback loop where the agent can learn from user interactions and improve its decision-making over time.

Best Practice: Ensure that AI agents are constantly learning and evolving based on user data, business changes, and new technological advancements.

⬜ 6. Implement Strong Data Governance and Ethical Standards

AI agents rely heavily on data to make decisions. As such, **data governance** is crucial to ensure data integrity, privacy, and compliance with regulations. Additionally, ethical considerations must be central to AI agent development.

- **Data Privacy**: Ensure that sensitive data, such as personally identifiable information (PII), is protected and that data is processed in accordance with relevant privacy laws (e.g., GDPR, CCPA).

- **Bias Mitigation**: Work to eliminate biases in the training data. AI systems can inadvertently reinforce biases present in the data, so it's important to use diverse, representative data.

- **Transparency and Accountability**: Provide transparency about how AI decisions are made, especially in critical business processes. End users should be able to understand why the AI agent took a particular action or made a specific recommendation.

Best Practice: Regularly audit the data used for training AI agents and implement frameworks to ensure ethical decision-making.

7. Leverage ServiceNow's Built-in AI and Automation Tools

ServiceNow provides a powerful set of built-in **AI and automation tools** that can accelerate the development of AI agents. Utilize these tools to reduce development time, increase reliability, and ensure integration with the broader ServiceNow platform.

- **Virtual Agent Designer**: Use ServiceNow's Virtual Agent Designer to easily create and manage conversational AI agents. It offers templates and integration options for creating chatbots that work seamlessly with other ServiceNow modules.

- **AI Model Management**: Take advantage of ServiceNow's tools for managing machine learning (ML) models to ensure they are always optimized and evolving.

- **Performance Analytics**: Integrate performance analytics with AI agents to track success metrics and gather insights that can drive continuous improvement.

Best Practice: Leverage out-of-the-box capabilities to minimize custom development and ensure better compatibility with the platform's broader ecosystem.

8. Test, Monitor, and Optimize Continuously

AI agents require constant testing and monitoring to ensure they continue to meet business needs and user expectations. Continuous **optimization** is key to improving both performance and user experience.

- **Testing**: Perform thorough testing of AI agents, including functional, usability, and integration testing. Test how the agent handles edge cases, unexpected inputs, and errors.

- **Monitoring**: Set up monitoring to track AI agent performance, such as response time, accuracy, and customer satisfaction scores. This will allow you to spot any issues quickly and take corrective action.

- **Optimization**: Use insights from monitoring to improve the agent. If the AI is underperforming in certain areas, it may require retraining with new data or adjustments in algorithms.

Best Practice: Implement a monitoring and feedback system that allows AI agents to continuously adapt and optimize based on performance data.

9. Ensure Seamless Integration with Other Systems

AI agents should be integrated with other systems within your enterprise, such as CRM, ERP, and HR systems, to ensure they have access to the necessary data to make informed decisions. Integration enables AI agents to:

- **Access relevant data**: Ensure that AI agents can pull in data from other systems to provide accurate and contextually relevant responses.

- **Trigger cross-platform actions**: AI agents should be able to initiate actions in other systems, such as creating service requests or updating employee records, based on user inputs or system triggers.

- **Provide holistic experiences**: Integrated AI agents deliver a more cohesive experience across various business functions and processes.

Best Practice: Prioritize seamless integration and data flow across different systems to ensure that AI agents can deliver optimal performance across the organization.

10. Align AI Agent Development with Long-Term Strategy

Finally, it's essential to align AI agent development with your organization's **long-term digital transformation strategy**. The journey doesn't stop at development; ongoing support, scalability, and integration with future technologies must be considered.

- **Scalability**: Ensure the AI agents are built to scale as the organization grows. This includes planning for high volumes of users and data.

- **Future-proofing**: Keep an eye on emerging AI technologies, such as deep learning and reinforcement learning, to ensure that your AI agents remain competitive and relevant.

- **Strategic Alignment**: Regularly assess whether the AI agents are helping the organization meet its broader business and digital transformation goals.

Best Practice: Continuously revisit the strategic alignment of AI agents with your organizational goals and adjust as needed.

Conclusion: Building Future-Ready AI Agents

Building AI agents is not a one-off effort but an ongoing, iterative process that requires attention to business needs, user experience, and continuous improvement. By following these best practices, organizations can ensure that AI agents not only deliver immediate value but also contribute to long-term digital transformation goals.

Through a combination of careful design, strategic planning, and leveraging the right tools, ServiceNow's AI agents can become an essential part of an organization's future-ready technology stack.

CHAPTER 12: MEASURING SUCCESS AND ROI OF AI AGENTS

"Measuring the success of AI agents is not just about tracking performance metrics—it's about understanding their impact on business outcomes and continuously optimizing them to drive value."

1. Introduction to Measuring AI Agent Success and ROI

AI agents hold significant potential to drive efficiency, enhance customer experiences, and reduce operational costs. However, to ensure that these agents are genuinely creating value for the business, it's essential to have a clear framework for measuring their success and return on investment (ROI). This chapter discusses key performance indicators (KPIs), measurement strategies, and methods for assessing the long-term value of AI agents.

2. Define Clear Success Metrics and KPIs

The first step in measuring the success of AI agents is to define clear metrics and key performance indicators (KPIs) that align with business objectives. The right KPIs will depend on the specific use case and the goals of the AI agent but could include the following:

- **Customer Satisfaction (CSAT)**: Measure user satisfaction through surveys, ratings, and feedback after interactions with the AI agent. A high CSAT score typically indicates that the AI agent is meeting user expectations.

- **First Contact Resolution (FCR)**: Track the percentage of issues resolved by the AI agent in the first interaction without the need for human escalation. High FCR rates indicate that the AI is effective at solving common problems.

- **Average Handle Time (AHT)**: Measure how long it takes the AI agent to handle a request or issue. A lower AHT can indicate that the agent is efficient and streamlined.

- **Employee Productivity**: Evaluate the impact of the AI agent on employee productivity by measuring how much time is saved by automating repetitive tasks. This can be quantified in terms of time savings per employee.

- **Escalation Rate**: Track how often AI agents escalate tasks to human agents. A lower escalation rate suggests that the AI is capable of handling more complex queries.

Best Practice: Align success metrics with both short-term goals (e.g., faster response times) and long-term outcomes (e.g., improved user experience).

3. Understand the Business Impact of AI Agents

While technical metrics like FCR and AHT are essential, the real value of AI agents lies in their **business impact**. Consider these aspects:

- **Cost Reduction**: Measure how much operational

cost is saved by automating processes. AI agents can reduce the need for human intervention in routine tasks, leading to significant cost savings over time.

- **Revenue Growth**: Evaluate the potential for AI agents to drive revenue through upselling, cross-selling, or improving customer retention by providing quicker and more accurate service.

- **Operational Efficiency**: AI agents can streamline workflows by automating manual processes, reducing error rates, and improving decision-making. Measure the time and resources saved by AI automation in comparison to manual processing.

- **Customer Retention and Loyalty**: Evaluate the role AI agents play in enhancing customer experience, leading to greater satisfaction and improved loyalty. Happy customers are more likely to stay and engage with your brand.

Best Practice: In addition to tracking operational metrics, assess the broader impact on business outcomes to understand the ROI of AI agents.

☐ 4. Measure AI Agent Performance with Data Analytics

AI agents generate vast amounts of data that can be used to measure their performance and make informed decisions about improvements. Leveraging data analytics tools helps uncover insights into the agent's effectiveness and areas for optimization.

- **Behavioral Analytics**: Track how users interact with the AI agent, including common queries, response times, and engagement rates. Identify patterns that indicate friction points or gaps in the agent's capabilities.

- **Machine Learning (ML) Feedback Loop**: Use feedback from users to continuously train the AI agent. Monitor how the agent improves its responses over time based on the feedback and interactions with users.

- **Root Cause Analysis**: When the AI agent fails to resolve an issue, perform a root cause analysis to identify where the agent's logic or knowledge base needs improvement. This can guide ongoing training and refinements.

Best Practice: Leverage ServiceNow's Performance Analytics and ML capabilities to analyze AI agent performance data and feed this into optimization efforts.

⬜ 5. ROI Calculation Framework for AI Agents

Calculating the **ROI** of AI agents requires a comprehensive framework that looks beyond development and deployment costs. Key components of this calculation include:

- **Initial Development Costs**: The cost of building, testing, and deploying the AI agent, including platform costs and developer time.

- **Ongoing Maintenance Costs**: The cost of maintaining and updating the AI agent, including updates to training data, monitoring, and performance improvements.

- **Cost Savings**: Quantify the savings resulting from automation, such as reduced labor costs, fewer errors, and improved service efficiency.

- **Revenue Impact**: Estimate the incremental

revenue generated by AI agents, such as higher conversion rates, increased customer retention, and upselling opportunities.

- **Time to Value**: Measure how long it takes for the AI agent to achieve a positive ROI. This can be tracked by comparing the time taken to reach break-even (where benefits outweigh costs) and the long-term return over time.

Best Practice: Use a combination of qualitative and quantitative measures to calculate ROI, considering both direct financial benefits and operational improvements.

⬚ 6. Continuous Monitoring and Optimization

AI agents should not be treated as set-it-and-forget-it solutions. To maximize ROI, you need to engage in **continuous monitoring** and **optimization**:

- **Performance Dashboards**: Use dashboards to monitor AI agent performance in real-time. Key metrics to track include resolution time, customer satisfaction, and number of escalations.

- **User Feedback Loops:** Actively collect and analyze user feedback to identify areas where the agent needs improvement. This feedback can be collected through surveys, ratings, or direct user input.

- **Retrospective Analysis**: Periodically review AI agent performance to identify trends and assess whether the agent is meeting its objectives. This analysis should lead to targeted optimization efforts.

Best Practice: Implement a regular review cycle for evaluating AI agent performance, using both quantitative metrics and qualitative feedback to inform improvements.

☐ 7. Engage Stakeholders in Evaluating AI Success

Engage key stakeholders across the organization to evaluate the success of AI agents. This includes business leaders, process owners, and the IT team. Having cross-functional collaboration will ensure that the AI agent's performance is assessed from multiple perspectives:

- **Business Leaders**: Focus on how the AI agent aligns with strategic goals and delivers measurable outcomes.

- **IT and Development Teams**: Evaluate the technical performance, reliability, and scalability of the AI agents.

- **End Users**: Collect feedback from users who interact with the AI agent regularly to understand their experience and gather improvement suggestions.

Best Practice: Conduct regular stakeholder meetings to discuss AI agent performance, gather insights, and plan for iterative improvements.

☐ 8. Reporting on AI Agent ROI to Executives

Reporting AI agent success and ROI to executives is crucial for securing ongoing investment and support. When creating reports for senior leadership, ensure the following:

- **Clear Visualization of Metrics**: Use charts, graphs, and dashboards to present ROI metrics in an easily digestible format.

- **Contextualize with Business Impact**: Frame ROI results within the context of business objectives —such as how AI agents improved customer experience or saved operational costs.

- **Benchmarking Against Industry Standards**: Compare your AI agent's performance against industry benchmarks to show how it stacks up against peers.

Best Practice: Develop a comprehensive executive report that aligns AI agent performance with organizational goals, presenting both hard data and qualitative insights.

Conclusion: Driving Value with AI Agents

Measuring the success and ROI of AI agents is an ongoing process that requires careful attention to both quantitative and qualitative data. By using clear metrics, continuously optimizing performance, and assessing the broader business impact, organizations can ensure their AI agents deliver long-term value.

The future of AI in the enterprise is bright, and by aligning AI initiatives with strategic business goals, organizations can maximize the ROI of these cutting-edge technologies.

CHAPTER 13: THE FUTURE OF AI AGENTS AND THEIR ROLE IN DIGITAL TRANSFORMATION

"AI agents are not just tools; they are transformative technologies that will redefine how businesses operate and interact with their customers, partners, and employees in the years to come."

☐ 1. Introduction: AI Agents as Catalysts for Digital Transformation

The role of AI agents has evolved from simple task automation to becoming central players in an organization's digital transformation journey. With their ability to handle complex tasks, learn from interactions, and integrate into diverse business processes, AI agents are poised to drive the future of customer experiences, operations, and decision-making across industries.

In this chapter, we explore the future potential of AI agents, their expanding role in digital transformation, and how organizations can leverage them to stay ahead of the curve.

☐ 2. The Expanding Role of AI Agents in the Enterprise

As AI technology continues to evolve, the scope of AI agents' impact on organizations will grow significantly. The future will see AI agents transforming beyond just customer service and IT support to other critical areas of business:

- **Operational Automation**: AI agents will further automate back-office functions such as procurement, finance, and supply chain management, eliminating manual tasks and increasing efficiency.

- **Decision Support**: AI agents will assist decision-makers by analyzing data, predicting trends, and providing insights that enable more informed, data-driven decisions.

- **Hyper-Personalization**: AI agents will become key enablers of hyper-personalized customer experiences, tailoring interactions based on individual preferences, past behavior, and real-time data.

- **Proactive Engagement**: Future AI agents will not only respond to user queries but will also anticipate needs and proactively engage with users, improving both customer experience and operational efficiency.

Best Practice: Consider how AI agents can expand beyond their current role and integrate into broader business processes to maximize their transformative potential.

3. The Integration of AI Agents with Emerging Technologies

The future of AI agents will be closely tied to other emerging technologies, enhancing their capabilities and enabling new use cases:

- **5G Networks**: With the advent of 5G, AI agents

will be able to handle real-time data streams more effectively, enabling faster response times and more sophisticated applications, such as real-time customer support and autonomous systems.

- **IoT (Internet of Things)**: AI agents will become even more integrated with IoT devices, enabling smart environments where AI can manage everything from home automation to supply chain logistics, offering new opportunities for efficiency and convenience.

- **Blockchain**: AI agents will leverage blockchain technology to enhance security, transparency, and trust in applications like digital contracts, supply chain tracking, and financial transactions.

- **Augmented Reality (AR) and Virtual Reality (VR)**: AI agents will integrate with AR/VR environments to create immersive experiences, whether it's through virtual customer service representatives, AI-driven training, or interactive product demonstrations.

Best Practice: Stay ahead of the technological curve by integrating AI agents with emerging technologies to unlock new opportunities and enhance their capabilities.

4. The Evolution of Human-AI Collaboration

The future of AI agents isn't just about replacing human workers —it's about collaboration. As AI technology advances, human roles will shift to complement AI agents rather than compete with them:

- **AI as a Co-Worker**: In many sectors, AI agents will act as assistants to human workers, handling repetitive tasks while allowing employees to focus on more strategic, creative, and value-added activities. This will create a more efficient, hybrid work environment.

- **AI-Driven Augmentation**: AI will augment human decision-making by providing real-time insights, predictions, and recommendations that empower employees to make better-informed choices.

- **Empathy in AI**: As AI agents become more capable of understanding human emotions and contexts, they will collaborate with humans in ways that require empathy, such as offering emotional support in healthcare or providing a more personalized customer service experience.

Best Practice: Foster a culture of collaboration between AI agents and employees to maximize the value of both, driving higher productivity and innovation.

5. Ethical Considerations and Responsible AI Development

As AI agents become more integrated into business processes, it's crucial to consider the ethical implications of their use. Ensuring that AI is developed and deployed responsibly will be a key factor in their future success:

- **Bias and Fairness**: AI systems must be trained on diverse, representative datasets to avoid perpetuating bias. Companies will need to implement measures to ensure fairness in AI agent interactions and decisions.

- **Transparency**: AI agents should be transparent about how they make decisions, especially in high-stakes environments such as healthcare, finance, and law. Users must be able to understand why AI agents take certain actions or make particular recommendations.

- **Accountability**: As AI systems become more autonomous, clear accountability structures will be necessary to determine who is responsible for decisions made by AI agents.

- **Data Privacy**: Protecting user data and ensuring that AI agents comply with data protection regulations, such as GDPR, will be essential as AI continues to process more sensitive information.

Best Practice: Implement responsible AI development practices, focusing on transparency, fairness, and data privacy, to build trust with users and ensure ethical AI deployment.

6. AI Agents and the Future of Work

The future of work will be significantly influenced by AI agents. As more businesses adopt AI-driven automation, the workplace will evolve in several ways:

- **Reskilling and Upskilling**: AI will automate routine tasks, but humans will still play a critical role in managing, supervising, and improving AI systems. This will create a need for ongoing reskilling and upskilling programs to ensure that the workforce can adapt to new roles.

- **Workplace Evolution**: AI will facilitate flexible work environments, with AI agents supporting remote work, virtual collaboration, and employee well-being through wellness programs and mental health support.

- **AI-Enhanced Creativity**: In creative fields, AI agents will be able to assist with content generation, design, and other tasks that enhance creativity and innovation, working alongside humans rather than replacing them.

Best Practice: Prepare your workforce for the future of work by investing in reskilling programs and fostering a collaborative relationship between humans and AI.

☐ 7. Global Impact and Industry-Specific Applications

AI agents will continue to transform industries, each with unique applications and challenges. Some industry-specific opportunities include:

- **Healthcare**: AI agents will assist with patient care, medical diagnostics, and administrative tasks, improving outcomes and efficiency in healthcare settings.

- **Retail**: In retail, AI agents will offer personalized shopping experiences, streamline inventory management, and enhance customer service.

- **Finance**: AI agents will automate financial transactions, assist with compliance and fraud detection, and provide personalized financial advice to customers.

- **Manufacturing**: AI agents will enable predictive maintenance, optimize production lines, and improve supply chain logistics in manufacturing.

Best Practice: Tailor AI solutions to the unique needs of each industry to fully realize their potential and drive innovation.

☐ 8. Conclusion: Embracing the Future of AI Agents

AI agents are undeniably at the forefront of digital transformation, offering opportunities to drive business efficiency, enhance customer experiences, and enable new ways of working. By integrating AI into critical business processes and remaining proactive in adapting to emerging technologies, businesses can leverage AI agents to stay competitive and innovate continuously.

The future of AI agents is bright, and the journey to fully harness their potential will require strategic planning, ethical consideration, and a forward-thinking mindset.

CHAPTER 14: APPENDIX & REFERENCES

1. Useful Tools and Resources

To successfully deploy AI agents, you'll need access to a suite of tools and resources. Here's a list of essential ServiceNow tools and external resources that will support your development, deployment, and scaling efforts.

ServiceNow Tools for AI Agent Development

1. **AI Agent Designer**:
   The AI Agent Designer provides a visual interface for creating and configuring AI agent personas. This tool helps you define agent behaviors, conversational flows, and interactions with users.

2. **Predictive Intelligence**:
   ServiceNow's Predictive Intelligence tool leverages machine learning to automatically classify and assign incoming service requests based on historical data, improving incident resolution times and enhancing user experience.

3. **Virtual Agent Designer**:
   The Virtual Agent Designer allows users to create chatbots that can handle simple tasks, answer frequently asked questions, and guide users through workflows. These agents can be

connected to the broader platform for even more robust functionality.

4. **Natural Language Understanding (NLU)**:
   NLU is used to process and understand user input in natural language, helping AI agents interpret user queries and provide relevant responses.

5. **Now Assist**:
   Now Assist enables ServiceNow to integrate generative AI, leveraging advanced language models to provide sophisticated responses and problem-solving capabilities across various service domains (ITSM, HR, CSM, etc.).

6. **Performance Analytics**:
   Use Performance Analytics to monitor and evaluate the effectiveness of your AI agents. You can track KPIs such as resolution rates, user satisfaction, and containment rates to refine and improve agent performance.

7. **Governance, Risk, and Compliance (GRC)**:
   The GRC module ensures that your AI agents comply with organizational, regulatory, and ethical standards, offering tools for audit tracking, versioning, and transparency.

External AI and Data Integration Tools

1. **Hugging Face**:
   Hugging Face provides pre-trained models and tools for natural language processing, which can be integrated with ServiceNow's AI agents to enhance understanding and generation capabilities.

2. **Azure OpenAI**:
   Azure OpenAI services offer a scalable platform for deploying powerful AI models, including GPT-

based models. You can use this integration to scale the natural language capabilities of your ServiceNow AI agents.

3. **Google Cloud AI**:
   Google's AI services provide additional options for machine learning models, sentiment analysis, and advanced data processing. These tools can complement ServiceNow's AI capabilities for more nuanced interactions.

4. **IBM Watson**:
   IBM Watson's AI tools offer advanced capabilities in NLP, sentiment analysis, and AI-powered automation. ServiceNow integrates with Watson to enhance agent-driven conversational experiences.

5. **OpenAI GPT**:
   OpenAI's GPT models, such as GPT-4, provide sophisticated language generation capabilities. These can be integrated into ServiceNow to deliver intelligent, human-like conversations in AI agents.

2. Best Practices for AI Agent Development

When building AI agents on the ServiceNow platform, adopting best practices is critical for ensuring success. Here are some key best practices to keep in mind throughout the design, deployment, and scaling phases:

AI Agent Design Best Practices

1. **Define Clear Personas**:
   Ensure that each AI agent has a well-defined persona with clear boundaries, context, and user expectations. A well-crafted persona can increase trust and engagement with users.

2. **Use Modular Components**:

Design agents with modular components, such as intents, dialogs, and actions. This allows for easier updates and scalability over time.

3. **Ensure Seamless Integration with ServiceNow Modules**:
   Ensure that your AI agents are deeply integrated with ServiceNow's native modules like ITSM, HRSD, CSM, and others. This will enable the agents to leverage existing workflows and data, improving the overall experience.

4. **Use Real-World Data for Training**:
   Train AI agents on real-world enterprise data to ensure they can respond to practical scenarios effectively. Avoid training on overly generic data, as it can reduce the relevance and accuracy of responses.

5. **Design with Failover in Mind**:
   Always build in a failover mechanism to escalate to human agents when needed. The AI agent should be able to seamlessly hand off complex or sensitive cases to human counterparts.

AI Agent Governance and Ethics

1. **Bias Mitigation**:
   Ensure that your AI agents are trained on diverse datasets and that efforts are made to eliminate biases that could affect their interactions or decision-making.

2. **Transparent Decision-Making**:
   Enable explainability in the AI agent's actions. Users should be able to understand how and why certain decisions were made, particularly when it comes to high-stakes tasks.

3. **Data Privacy**:

Ensure that your AI agents comply with regional data protection laws (e.g., GDPR, CCPA) and that sensitive data is properly encrypted, anonymized, and stored securely.

4. **Compliance Monitoring**:
Use ServiceNow's built-in governance tools to track agent performance and compliance with legal, ethical, and organizational standards. Regular audits will ensure that AI agents remain compliant over time.

3. References

Here is a list of valuable references that will help you stay updated with the latest trends, research, and guidelines for implementing AI agents in your organization:

Books and Guides

- **"Artificial Intelligence: A Guide for Thinking Humans" by Melanie Mitchell**
This book offers an accessible and comprehensive overview of AI, from its history to its future, and is a great resource for understanding AI technology in general.

- **"AI Superpowers: China, Silicon Valley, and the New World Order" by Kai-Fu Lee**
A look into the AI arms race between China and the US, and the future of AI in various industries. A good read for understanding the global AI landscape.

- **"Architecting the Cloud" by Michael J. Kavis**
This book focuses on cloud architecture, providing insights into how AI and other cloud-native technologies are reshaping enterprise architecture.

Whitepapers and Articles

- **"The Role of AI in IT Service Management" (ServiceNow Whitepaper)**
  Learn how AI is being integrated into ITSM to improve service delivery and efficiency.

- **"Building Trust in AI: A Guide for Enterprise Leaders" (Harvard Business Review)**
  An essential resource for understanding how to build and maintain trust in AI systems.

Online Communities and Forums

- **ServiceNow Community**
  Join the ServiceNow community to engage with other professionals, share ideas, and stay up to date with the latest product updates and best practices.

- **AI Alignment Forum**
  Participate in discussions on the ethical, technical, and social aspects of AI to stay informed about responsible AI practices.

- **Hugging Face Forums**
  Engage with AI experts and practitioners to explore NLP, transformers, and AI model development topics.

---

4. Next Steps: Building Your AI Agent Roadmap

In this chapter, we have discussed essential tools, resources, and best practices for AI agent development on the ServiceNow platform. To move forward, you should:

1. Review your current AI agent strategy and identify areas for improvement or expansion.

2. Implement the tools and best practices mentioned to enhance your AI agents' capabilities.

3. Stay updated on emerging technologies and adjust your roadmap as new developments arise.

4. Establish a continuous learning cycle, monitoring agent performance and user feedback to refine their effectiveness.

Absolutely! Let's create a detailed roadmap for building an AI agent strategy, keeping in mind a futuristic vision and the maturity model for the AI Agent ecosystem. The goal is to align this roadmap with today's transformation needs and business outcomes.

Building Your AI Agent Roadmap: A Futuristic Vision for Business Transformation

An AI Agent roadmap is not just a plan to implement AI agents but a strategic framework to evolve your enterprise's capabilities over time. It reflects an evolving vision of how AI can drive smarter business processes, transform workflows, and enable businesses to scale intelligently. The key is to leverage a structured maturity model and to align each phase of your AI roadmap with your long-term business outcomes.

Here's a breakdown of how to approach this roadmap with a focus on the **futuristic vision** and the **maturity model**.

1. Visionary Goals: Defining the AI Agent Future

Before diving into tactical steps, define the high-level futuristic vision for AI agents in your organization. This vision will provide direction, ensure alignment with business goals, and guide the platform's evolution.

Futuristic Vision for AI Agents in Your Organization:

- **Autonomous AI Agents**: The ultimate goal is to create AI agents that can autonomously perform tasks, learn from interactions, and make decisions without human intervention. These agents will drive operational efficiencies, perform predictive tasks, and even take corrective actions across workflows.

- **Multidomain Interoperability**: AI agents will seamlessly operate across various domains (ITSM, HRSD, CSM, SecOps) and integrate with other business systems, breaking down silos and facilitating cross-functional automation.

- **Real-Time Decision Making**: The ability to adapt in real-time to changing business conditions and data inputs will be central. AI agents will analyze incoming data, predict outcomes, and act instantaneously to optimize workflows.

- **Human-AI Collaboration**: Instead of replacing humans, AI agents will collaborate with employees, handling routine tasks and offering decision-making support, allowing humans to focus on higher-value activities.

- **Ethical AI and Governance**: The AI agents will evolve in a transparent, explainable, and ethical framework, ensuring that business decisions made by AI agents align with corporate values and comply with regional data privacy regulations.

2. Building the AI Agent Maturity Model

An AI Agent Maturity Model serves as a key framework for measuring your organization's progress in developing AI-driven solutions. The model should assess the current state of AI adoption and guide you toward higher maturity levels, enabling businesses to scale their AI capabilities over time.

AI Agent Maturity Model: Stages of Development

1. **Stage 1: Initial (Exploration and Proof of Concept)**

   - **Focus**: Experimenting with AI agents on a small scale to understand the technology.

   - **Key Activities**: Proof of Concept (PoC), early pilot projects, testing basic virtual agents for simple tasks like FAQ resolution and service requests.

   - **Business Outcome**: Initial insights into AI's potential, foundational training of agents, and basic understanding of user interactions.

   - **Key Challenges**: Limited AI capability, manual intervention required, inconsistent results, high initial costs.

Key Metrics:

   - Agent Resolution Rate: 10-20%

   - User Satisfaction (CSAT): Below 4/5

2. **Stage 2: Emerging (Early Adoption and Deployment)**

   - **Focus**: Expanding the deployment of AI agents to handle routine tasks, such as ticket classification, categorization, and basic customer service.

   - **Key Activities**: Creating and deploying multiple agents across departments like ITSM, HR, and CSM. Beginning to automate more routine workflows with integration to the ServiceNow platform.

   - **Business Outcome**: Improved process efficiency, faster response times, and better resource allocation.

- **Key Challenges**: Resistance to change, managing complexity across departments, limited agent knowledge.

Key Metrics:

- Agent Resolution Rate: 30-40%

- First Contact Resolution (FCR): 50%

- CSAT: 4.0-4.3/5

3. **Stage 3: Scaling (Enterprise-Wide Adoption)**
   - **Focus**: Scaling AI agents across multiple use cases and departments, with increasing autonomy and reduced need for human intervention.

   - **Key Activities**: Building an AI Agent Factory with reusable personas, knowledge models, and workflows. Integrating agents into a wide range of processes and enabling them to handle complex queries or predictive tasks.

   - **Business Outcome**: Increased productivity and scalability across departments. AI-driven decision-making.

   - **Key Challenges**: Data silos, platform integration complexities, governance issues.

Key Metrics:

- Agent Resolution Rate: 50-60%

- Containment Rate (no human

intervention): 70-80%

- CSAT: 4.3-4.5/5

- ROI: Increased efficiency and reduced cost per service.

4. **Stage 4: Optimized (AI Agent Ecosystem with Continuous Learning)**
    - **Focus**: AI agents that continuously learn from interactions, adapt autonomously, and make real-time decisions based on business needs.

    - **Key Activities**: Implementing machine learning and reinforcement learning models for continuous agent improvement. Expanding AI agents to perform predictive tasks like proactive service request creation, anomaly detection, and self-healing.

    - **Business Outcome**: Proactive problem solving, intelligent automation, continuous optimization of processes.

    - **Key Challenges**: Ensuring the ethical use of AI, managing trust and governance, scaling continuous learning models.

Key Metrics:

- Agent Resolution Rate: 70-80%

- Autonomous Task Completion: 80-90%

- CSAT: 4.5/5 and above

- ROI: Major reductions in operational costs and significant improvement in productivity.

5. **Stage 5: Autonomous (Fully Autonomous AI Agents)**

  - **Focus**: Agents that autonomously handle complex workflows across all business units without human intervention.

  - **Key Activities**: Advanced reinforcement learning and cross-agent collaboration. Full agent autonomy in critical business functions like IT operations, finance, HR, etc.

  - **Business Outcome**: Operationally intelligent, self-sustaining workflows with minimal human oversight.

  - **Key Challenges**: Regulatory compliance, high complexity in agent governance, continual need for AI explainability.

Key Metrics:

  - Autonomous Task Completion: 90% and above

  - Operational Costs: Significantly reduced due to full automation

  - Real-Time Decision Accuracy: > 95%

3. Creating Your AI Agent Roadmap: The Strategic Framework

The AI Agent roadmap should align with the **maturity model** and **futuristic vision**, ensuring that your platform evolves in a structured, scalable, and sustainable way. Below is a detailed framework to guide the creation of your roadmap:

Phase 1: Strategy Development (Short-Term – 0-6 Months)

- **Focus**: Set clear goals and objectives for AI implementation.

- **Key Activities**:
  - Define the business case and expected outcomes from AI adoption.
  - Conduct a maturity assessment to understand your starting point.
  - Identify the key business areas where AI agents can add immediate value (e.g., automating ticket classification, handling FAQs).
  - Initiate a Proof of Concept (PoC) for a selected use case.

- **Outcome**: Clear strategy and measurable KPIs for AI success.

Phase 2: AI Agent Design & Development (Medium-Term – 6-12 Months)

- **Focus**: Begin the design, development, and deployment of AI agents.

- **Key Activities**:
  - Build and prototype AI agents using tools like ServiceNow's AI Agent Designer.
  - Integrate AI agents into existing workflows across ITSM, HRSD, and CSM.
  - Test agent performance with real data and business scenarios.
  - Start using NLP, NLU, and AI models to improve agent decision-making.

- **Outcome**: Launch the first set of AI agents in

production with clear performance indicators.

Phase 3: Scaling & Continuous Improvement (Long-Term – 12-24 Months)

- **Focus**: Expand the deployment and ensure scalability.

- **Key Activities**:
  - Scale AI agents to handle a wider range of tasks, including predictive maintenance and proactive service delivery.

  - Leverage feedback loops and continuous learning to improve agent accuracy and decision-making.

  - Ensure robust governance for monitoring, compliance, and ethical AI usage.

- **Outcome**: Fully functional, scalable AI agent ecosystem with enterprise-wide adoption.

Phase 4: Autonomous AI & Optimization (Long-Term – 24+ Months)

- **Focus**: Achieve full autonomy and optimization in AI-powered workflows.

- **Key Activities**:
  - Implement advanced AI models like reinforcement learning for continuous adaptation.

  - Enable agents to proactively initiate tasks based on predicted business needs.

  - Integrate AI agents across multi-platform ecosystems for seamless collaboration.

- **Outcome**: AI-driven intelligent enterprise with autonomous workflows and real-time decision-making.

---

4. Transformational Impact & Business Outcomes

An AI Agent roadmap, designed with a futuristic vision and guided by a maturity model, helps your organization achieve the following:

- **Cost Reduction**: Through the automation of routine tasks, AI agents reduce the need for manual intervention, improving cost efficiency.

- **Operational Efficiency**: AI agents improve the speed and accuracy of service delivery, reducing response and resolution times.

- **Employee Productivity**: By taking over repetitive tasks, AI agents free employees to focus on more strategic, higher-value work.

- **Proactive Service Delivery**: With predictive capabilities, AI agents anticipate issues before they occur and proactively resolve problems, enhancing user satisfaction

- **Scalable Growth**: AI agents allow organizations to scale their operations without proportional increases in cost or resource requirements.

This **AI Agent Roadmap** will enable your organization to transform its operations, adopt cutting-edge AI technologies, and ultimately deliver superior business outcomes.

Certainly! Below is a structured list of **100 AI agent use cases** that could be included in your next chapter. These use cases span various industries, departments, and operational needs. Each use case includes a title, description, business outcome, and sample KPIs.

CHAPTER 16 : TOP 100 AI AGENT USE CASES FOR BUSINESS TRANSFORMATION

1. IT INCIDENT MANAGEMENT AUTOMATION

- **Description**: Automates the identification, categorization, prioritization, and resolution of IT incidents.

- **Business Outcome**: Faster resolution times, fewer errors, and cost reduction.

- **Sample KPI**: Incident handling time reduced by 30%, 80% first-contact resolution.

2. VIRTUAL HR ASSISTANT

- **Description**: AI-powered assistant that automates HR-related queries and tasks such as leave requests, payroll inquiries, and benefits management.

- **Business Outcome**: Streamlined HR operations, improved employee satisfaction, and reduced HR workload.

- **Sample KPI**: 90% employee satisfaction, 70% reduction in HR manual queries.

3. PROACTIVE CUSTOMER SUPPORT

- **Description**: AI agents proactively reach out to customers for updates, issues, or feedback.

- **Business Outcome**: Higher customer satisfaction and reduced case volume.

- **Sample KPI**: 35% increase in CSAT, 20% reduction in case escalation.

4. AUTOMATED KNOWLEDGE MANAGEMENT

- **Description**: AI agents help to manage, classify, and update knowledge articles based on usage patterns and new information.
- **Business Outcome**: More accurate and accessible knowledge base, reducing time spent searching for information.
- **Sample KPI**: Knowledge accuracy of 90%, 30% reduction in search time.

5. AI-DRIVEN IT CHANGE MANAGEMENT

- **Description**: AI agents analyze historical data to predict and mitigate risks associated with IT changes.

- **Business Outcome**: Reduced IT service disruptions and more effective change management.

- **Sample KPI**: 90% change success rate, 30% reduction in unplanned outages.

6. AI-POWERED CHATBOTS FOR CUSTOMER SUPPORT

- **Description**: Deploy AI chatbots to resolve common customer issues and provide 24/7 support.
- **Business Outcome**: Enhanced customer experience with faster response times and reduced reliance on human agents.
- **Sample KPI**: 90% customer satisfaction, 80% deflection of common inquiries.

7. PREDICTIVE ANALYTICS FOR IT OPERATIONS

- **Description**: AI analyzes infrastructure data to predict potential failures and service outages.

- **Business Outcome**: Proactive maintenance, reduced downtime, and improved system reliability.

- **Sample KPI**: 40% reduction in downtime, 25% improvement in predictive accuracy.

8. IT ASSET MANAGEMENT OPTIMIZATION

- **Description**: AI agents track the lifecycle of IT assets, ensuring compliance and optimal asset utilization.

- **Business Outcome**: Improved asset management, reduced operational risks, and better compliance.

- **Sample KPI**: 95% asset accuracy, 25% increase in asset utilization.

9. AI FOR CYBERSECURITY OPERATIONS (SECOPS)

- **Description**: AI automates the identification, categorization, and prioritization of security threats and incidents.

- **Business Outcome**: Reduced response time and improved security posture.

- **Sample KPI**: 50% faster response times, 20% reduction in false positives.

10. INTELLIGENT SERVICE REQUEST MANAGEMENT

- **Description**: AI automates the processing, approval, and fulfillment of standard service requests like access management.

- **Business Outcome**: Faster request fulfillment, reduced administrative overhead.

- **Sample KPI**: 70% request containment rate, 50% faster service request completion.

11. AI FOR SALES LEAD SCORING

- **Description**: AI analyzes historical sales data to assign scores to leads, helping sales teams prioritize high-value prospects.

- **Business Outcome**: Higher conversion rates and improved sales focus.

- **Sample KPI**: 20% increase in lead conversion rates, 15% increase in sales pipeline velocity.

12. AI-POWERED MARKETING CAMPAIGN OPTIMIZATION

- **Description**: AI analyzes marketing campaign performance and suggests optimizations in real-time.

- **Business Outcome**: Higher ROI on marketing spend and more effective campaigns.

- **Sample KPI**: 25% increase in campaign engagement, 15% improvement in conversion rates.

13. INTELLIGENT SUPPLY CHAIN MANAGEMENT

- **Description**: AI optimizes supply chain operations by predicting demand, optimizing routes, and reducing costs.
- **Business Outcome**: Reduced logistics costs and better inventory management.
- **Sample KPI**: 30% reduction in inventory costs, 20% improvement in supply chain efficiency.

14. AI-DRIVEN CUSTOMER SEGMENTATION

- **Description**: AI segments customers into groups based on their behavior, preferences, and purchasing history.

- **Business Outcome**: Targeted marketing and improved customer engagement.

- **Sample KPI**: 15% increase in customer retention, 20% improvement in sales per segment.

15. AI-POWERED FRAUD DETECTION IN FINANCE

- **Description**: AI identifies suspicious patterns in financial transactions to prevent fraud.
- **Business Outcome**: Reduced fraud rates and minimized financial loss.
- **Sample KPI**: 90% fraud detection rate, 40% reduction in false positives.

16. PREDICTIVE MAINTENANCE FOR MANUFACTURING

- **Description**: AI predicts equipment failure in manufacturing operations, enabling preventive maintenance.

- **Business Outcome**: Reduced downtime, extended equipment life, and cost savings.

- **Sample KPI**: 30% reduction in downtime, 20% reduction in maintenance costs.

17. PERSONALIZED E-COMMERCE RECOMMENDATIONS

- **Description**: AI recommends products based on customer browsing history and preferences.

- **Business Outcome**: Increased sales and customer engagement.

- **Sample KPI**: 25% increase in average order value, 30% increase in click-through rates.

18. AI FOR LEGAL DOCUMENT REVIEW

- **Description**: AI automates the review of legal documents, identifying key clauses and potential issues.

- **Business Outcome**: Faster legal document processing and reduced legal costs.

- **Sample KPI**: 40% reduction in document review time, 95% accuracy rate in identifying key clauses.

19. AI-POWERED RECRUITMENT ASSISTANT

- **Description**: AI screens resumes, schedules interviews, and assists with candidate evaluations in the recruitment process.

- **Business Outcome**: Faster hiring process and better candidate selection.

- **Sample KPI**: 50% reduction in time-to-hire, 80% accuracy in candidate match.

20. AI FOR FINANCIAL FORECASTING

- **Description**: AI models financial trends, providing forecasts for budgeting and resource allocation.

- **Business Outcome**: Better financial decision-making and more accurate forecasts.

- **Sample KPI**: 95% forecast accuracy, 10% increase in budget utilization efficiency.

21. AI FOR CUSTOMER SENTIMENT ANALYSIS

- **Description**: AI analyzes customer feedback, social media, and reviews to determine overall sentiment.

- **Business Outcome**: Improved product development and better customer service.

- **Sample KPI**: 80% sentiment accuracy, 25% improvement in customer satisfaction.

22. AI-POWERED PREDICTIVE HIRING

- **Description**: AI analyzes employee performance data to predict hiring needs and make staffing decisions.

- **Business Outcome**: More strategic workforce planning and optimized staffing.

- **Sample KPI**: 20% reduction in hiring costs, 15% improvement in employee retention.

23. AI-POWERED EXPENSE MANAGEMENT

- **Description**: AI categorizes and tracks business expenses, automating approval processes.

- **Business Outcome**: Reduced administrative overhead and improved financial compliance.

- **Sample KPI**: 25% reduction in expense processing time, 90% approval accuracy.

24. AI FOR PERSONALIZED EDUCATION AND TRAINING

- **Description**: AI provides personalized learning paths for employees, recommending training based on performance and career goals.

- **Business Outcome**: Enhanced employee development and skill acquisition.

- **Sample KPI**: 30% improvement in employee performance, 20% increase in training completion rates.

25. SMART CITY TRAFFIC MANAGEMENT

- **Description**: AI optimizes traffic flow in urban environments, reducing congestion and improving transportation efficiency.

- **Business Outcome**: Reduced traffic congestion and improved public transport efficiency.

- **Sample KPI**: 20% reduction in traffic congestion, 15% reduction in commute times.

26. AI-POWERED ENERGY CONSUMPTION OPTIMIZATION

- **Description**: AI optimizes energy usage in buildings and factories by analyzing real-time consumption data.

- **Business Outcome**: Reduced energy costs and improved sustainability.

- **Sample KPI**: 15% reduction in energy consumption, 10% cost savings.

27. AI FOR HEALTHCARE DIAGNOSIS ASSISTANCE

- **Description**: AI assists doctors by analyzing medical images, lab results, and patient data to suggest diagnoses.

- **Business Outcome**: Faster, more accurate diagnoses and improved patient outcomes.

- **Sample KPI**: 25% reduction in diagnostic errors, 15% improvement in patient satisfaction.

28. AI-DRIVEN INVENTORY OPTIMIZATION

- **Description**: AI manages inventory levels in real-time, predicting stockouts and optimizing stock levels.
- **Business Outcome**: Reduced stockouts and overstock situations, improving cash flow.
- **Sample KPI**: 20% reduction in stockouts, 15% improvement in inventory turnover.

29. AI FOR REAL-TIME COMPLIANCE MONITORING

- **Description**: AI monitors transactions and operations in real-time to ensure compliance with industry regulations.

- **Business Outcome**: Improved compliance and reduced risk of penalties.

- **Sample KPI**: 100% compliance rate, 25% reduction in audit costs.

30. AI FOR REAL-TIME TRANSLATION SERVICES

- **Description**: AI provides real-time translation for global teams, improving communication across languages.

- **Business Outcome**: Improved collaboration and communication in multilingual teams.

- **Sample KPI**: 30% improvement in communication efficiency, 95% translation accuracy.

31. AI-POWERED SOCIAL MEDIA MONITORING

- **Description**: AI monitors social media platforms for brand mentions, customer sentiment, and trending topics.

- **Business Outcome**: Enhanced brand reputation management and faster response to customer feedback.

- **Sample KPI**: 25% increase in engagement, 30% faster response time to customer mentions.

32. AI-DRIVEN DOCUMENT CLASSIFICATION

- **Description**: AI automatically categorizes documents based on their content, making it easier to find and manage them.

- **Business Outcome**: Improved document organization and retrieval times.

- **Sample KPI**: 90% classification accuracy, 40% reduction in document search time.

33. AI FOR LEGAL CONTRACT ANALYSIS

- **Description**: AI helps legal teams by identifying key clauses, risks, and terms in contracts.

- **Business Outcome**: Faster contract review and reduced legal risks.

- **Sample KPI**: 50% reduction in contract review time, 80% accuracy in risk detection.

34. AI-DRIVEN FINANCIAL RISK ASSESSMENT

- **Description**: AI analyzes financial transactions and external data to assess the potential risk of investments.
- **Business Outcome**: Better financial decision-making and improved investment strategies.
- **Sample KPI**: 20% reduction in financial risks, 10% improvement in investment returns.

35. AI FOR CUSTOMER JOURNEY MAPPING

- **Description**: AI analyzes customer interactions across touchpoints to map their journey and identify friction points.
- **Business Outcome**: Optimized customer experience and improved customer retention.
- **Sample KPI**: 15% increase in customer retention, 20% reduction in customer churn.

36. AI-POWERED SALES FORECASTING

- **Description**: AI analyzes historical sales data to predict future sales trends and adjust strategies accordingly.

- **Business Outcome**: More accurate sales forecasts and optimized resource allocation.

- **Sample KPI**: 10% improvement in forecast accuracy, 15% increase in sales performance.

37. AI-ENHANCED VIRTUAL PERSONAL ASSISTANT

- **Description**: AI-powered virtual assistant to help employees with scheduling, reminders, and task management.

- **Business Outcome**: Increased productivity and time saved on administrative tasks.

- **Sample KPI**: 30% reduction in time spent on scheduling, 20% improvement in task completion rate.

38. PREDICTIVE ANALYTICS FOR CUSTOMER CHURN

- **Description**: AI identifies patterns that predict customer churn and suggests interventions to retain high-risk customers.

- **Business Outcome**: Reduced churn and improved customer loyalty.

- **Sample KPI**: 15% reduction in churn rate, 10% increase in customer retention.

39. AI-POWERED DYNAMIC PRICING

- **Description**: AI adjusts prices in real-time based on market demand, competition, and customer behavior.

- **Business Outcome**: Optimized pricing strategies and improved profitability.

- **Sample KPI**: 10% increase in profit margins, 20% increase in sales revenue.

40. AI FOR HEALTHCARE PATIENT MONITORING

- **Description**: AI monitors patient health metrics in real-time and alerts healthcare providers to potential issues.

- **Business Outcome**: Improved patient outcomes and reduced hospital readmission rates.

- **Sample KPI**: 30% reduction in hospital readmissions, 15% improvement in patient outcomes.

41. AI FOR AUTOMATED FINANCIAL AUDITING

- **Description**: AI automates the process of auditing financial transactions and identifying anomalies or compliance issues.

- **Business Outcome**: Reduced audit time and improved financial accuracy.

- **Sample KPI**: 40% reduction in audit time, 25% improvement in financial accuracy.

42. AI-POWERED SUPPLY CHAIN FORECASTING

- **Description**: AI predicts demand and optimizes supply chain decisions, reducing waste and improving operational efficiency.
- **Business Outcome**: Improved inventory management and reduced supply chain disruptions.
- **Sample KPI**: 20% reduction in stockouts, 15% improvement in on-time deliveries.

43. AI-DRIVEN CHATBOT FOR HEALTHCARE SUPPORT

- **Description**: AI chatbot for providing immediate medical advice, appointment scheduling, and prescription refills.

- **Business Outcome**: Improved patient experience and reduced strain on healthcare professionals.

- **Sample KPI**: 30% reduction in appointment scheduling time, 20% increase in patient satisfaction.

44. AI FOR MANUFACTURING PROCESS OPTIMIZATION

- **Description**: AI optimizes production processes by analyzing equipment performance and material flow.

- **Business Outcome**: Increased manufacturing efficiency and reduced operational costs.

- **Sample KPI**: 15% increase in production output, 10% reduction in operational costs.

45. AI-POWERED DOCUMENT AUTOMATION

- **Description**: AI automates document creation by analyzing data and generating required documents like reports and contracts.

- **Business Outcome**: Reduced manual effort and faster document processing.

- **Sample KPI**: 50% reduction in document creation time, 95% accuracy in document content.

46. AI FOR PREDICTIVE CUSTOMER SUPPORT

- **Description**: AI predicts customer issues based on historical data and proactively offers solutions.

- **Business Outcome**: Reduced customer support load and improved customer satisfaction.

- **Sample KPI**: 20% reduction in support cases, 15% improvement in CSAT scores.

47. AI-DRIVEN SALES COACHING

- **Description**: AI analyzes sales conversations and performance data to provide personalized coaching to sales representatives.

- **Business Outcome**: Improved sales performance and more effective sales strategies.

- **Sample KPI**: 15% increase in sales performance, 20% improvement in deal conversion rate.

48. AI FOR SMART CONTRACT MANAGEMENT

- **Description**: AI helps create, track, and enforce smart contracts by automating verification and compliance checks.

- **Business Outcome**: Increased transparency, efficiency, and trust in contractual agreements.

- **Sample KPI**: 25% reduction in contract negotiation time, 95% reduction in contract disputes.

49. AI FOR REAL-TIME DEMAND FORECASTING

- **Description**: AI predicts real-time product demand, allowing businesses to adjust production and inventory levels accordingly.

- **Business Outcome**: Optimized stock levels and reduced out-of-stock situations.

- **Sample KPI**: 15% reduction in inventory costs, 25% improvement in product availability.

50. AI-POWERED SENTIMENT ANALYSIS FOR BRAND MONITORING

- **Description**: AI analyzes customer reviews, social media, and online forums to gauge public sentiment about a brand.

- **Business Outcome**: Improved brand management and proactive customer service.

- **Sample KPI**: 20% increase in positive sentiment, 30% reduction in negative mentions.

51. AI FOR PREDICTING EQUIPMENT FAILURES

- **Description**: AI predicts failures in machinery by analyzing operational data and identifying patterns leading to breakdowns.
- **Business Outcome**: Reduced unplanned downtime and maintenance costs.
- **Sample KPI**: 30% reduction in downtime, 15% improvement in equipment lifespan.

52. AI-DRIVEN CUSTOMER FEEDBACK ANALYSIS

- **Description**: AI analyzes customer feedback from surveys, reviews, and social media to provide actionable insights.

- **Business Outcome**: Improved product and service offerings and higher customer satisfaction.

- **Sample KPI**: 25% increase in customer satisfaction, 20% reduction in negative feedback.

53. AI-POWERED CONTENT PERSONALIZATION

- **Description**: AI delivers personalized content to users based on browsing history, preferences, and behavior.

- **Business Outcome**: Increased engagement and customer loyalty.

- **Sample KPI**: 15% increase in content engagement, 10% improvement in customer retention.

54. AI FOR RISK MANAGEMENT IN FINANCIAL MARKETS

- **Description**: AI predicts financial market trends and identifies high-risk assets.
- **Business Outcome**: Better decision-making and reduced exposure to market volatility.
- **Sample KPI**: 10% improvement in risk-adjusted returns, 20% reduction in portfolio risk.

55. AI-DRIVEN PERSONALIZED LEARNING FOR EMPLOYEES

- **Description**: AI recommends tailored training and learning materials based on employees' performance and career goals.

- **Business Outcome**: Enhanced employee skill sets and career development.

- **Sample KPI**: 30% improvement in employee performance, 20% increase in training participation.

56. AI FOR AUTOMATED CONTENT GENERATION

- **Description**: AI generates content for blogs, social media, and marketing materials based on keywords and objectives.

- **Business Outcome**: Faster content production and enhanced marketing outreach.

- **Sample KPI**: 50% reduction in content creation time, 25% increase in content engagement.

57. AI FOR ENERGY GRID OPTIMIZATION

- **Description**: AI optimizes the distribution of energy across grids, adjusting supply based on demand and weather conditions.

- **Business Outcome**: Reduced energy costs and enhanced sustainability.

- **Sample KPI**: 15% reduction in energy waste, 20% improvement in grid stability.

58. AI FOR PREDICTIVE WORKFORCE SCHEDULING

- **Description**: AI optimizes workforce scheduling based on demand, employee availability, and performance data.

- **Business Outcome**: Increased workforce efficiency and reduced labor costs.

- **Sample KPI**: 20% reduction in overtime costs, 25% improvement in employee productivity.

59. AI-POWERED CLAIMS PROCESSING FOR INSURANCE

- **Description**: AI automates the assessment and processing of insurance claims, improving accuracy and reducing processing time.

- **Business Outcome**: Faster claims resolution and reduced operational costs.

- **Sample KPI**: 40% reduction in claims processing time, 25% improvement in claims accuracy.

60. AI-DRIVEN PERSONAL FINANCE MANAGEMENT

- **Description**: AI assists customers with managing their finances, budgeting, and predicting future expenses.
- **Business Outcome**: Enhanced customer financial literacy and satisfaction.
- **Sample KPI**: 30% increase in app engagement, 15% improvement in customer retention.

61. AI FOR FRAUD DETECTION IN E-COMMERCE

- **Description**: AI analyzes transaction patterns to identify potential fraudulent activities in real-time.

- **Business Outcome**: Reduced fraud risk and enhanced security for online transactions.

- **Sample KPI**: 40% reduction in fraudulent transactions, 15% decrease in chargeback rates.

62. AI-POWERED VIDEO ANALYTICS FOR SURVEILLANCE

- **Description**: AI analyzes video footage from surveillance cameras to detect suspicious activity and prevent crimes.

- **Business Outcome**: Enhanced security and reduced response time to incidents.

- **Sample KPI**: 30% reduction in security incidents, 20% faster response time to threats.

63. AI FOR PREDICTIVE HEALTHCARE DIAGNOSTICS

- **Description**: AI analyzes patient data to predict potential health issues and suggest preventive measures.

- **Business Outcome**: Improved patient care and reduced healthcare costs.

- **Sample KPI**: 25% reduction in hospital readmissions, 30% improvement in diagnostic accuracy.

64. AI-DRIVEN MARKET BASKET ANALYSIS

- **Description**: AI identifies patterns in customer purchasing behavior to predict items that are frequently bought together.

- **Business Outcome**: Improved cross-selling and upselling strategies.

- **Sample KPI**: 20% increase in average order value, 10% improvement in sales conversion.

65. AI FOR REAL-TIME TRAFFIC MANAGEMENT

- **Description**: AI adjusts traffic signals and routes in real-time to optimize traffic flow based on traffic conditions and patterns.

- **Business Outcome**: Reduced traffic congestion and improved urban mobility.

- **Sample KPI**: 25% reduction in traffic congestion, 15% decrease in commute times.

66. AI-POWERED EMPLOYEE WELLNESS PROGRAMS

- **Description**: AI provides personalized wellness recommendations based on employees' health data, promoting a healthier workforce.

- **Business Outcome**: Improved employee well-being and reduced absenteeism.

- **Sample KPI**: 20% reduction in employee absenteeism, 10% improvement in employee health metrics.

67. AI FOR CUSTOMER SEGMENTATION AND TARGETING

- **Description**: AI segments customers based on behavior, preferences, and demographics for targeted marketing.

- **Business Outcome**: Increased marketing effectiveness and ROI.

- **Sample KPI**: 15% increase in conversion rates, 20% improvement in marketing ROI.

68. AI-DRIVEN CONTENT CURATION FOR MEDIA

- **Description**: AI curates personalized content for users based on their interests and viewing habits.

- **Business Outcome**: Improved user engagement and satisfaction.

- **Sample KPI**: 25% increase in content consumption, 20% improvement in user retention.

69. AI FOR AUTOMATED DATA ENTRY

- **Description**: AI automates the extraction of data from forms, emails, and documents, eliminating manual data entry.

- **Business Outcome**: Reduced data entry errors and improved operational efficiency.

- **Sample KPI**: 40% reduction in data entry time, 10% improvement in data accuracy.

70. AI-POWERED RISK DETECTION FOR CYBERSECURITY

- **Description**: AI analyzes network traffic and behavior patterns to detect potential security threats and breaches.

- **Business Outcome**: Enhanced cybersecurity and reduced risk of data breaches.

- **Sample KPI**: 30% reduction in security incidents, 25% improvement in threat detection speed.

71. AI FOR AUTOMATED VOICE TRANSCRIPTION

- **Description**: AI transcribes audio and video recordings into text with high accuracy.
- **Business Outcome**: Improved productivity and accessibility.
- **Sample KPI**: 90% transcription accuracy, 50% reduction in transcription time.

72. AI-DRIVEN PRODUCT RECOMMENDATION ENGINES

- **Description**: AI uses customer data and behavior to recommend products that are likely to be of interest.

- **Business Outcome**: Increased sales and improved customer experience.

- **Sample KPI**: 25% increase in product recommendations, 15% improvement in customer conversion rate.

73. AI FOR PREDICTIVE MAINTENANCE IN AUTOMOTIVE INDUSTRY

- **Description**: AI analyzes vehicle data to predict when maintenance is required, reducing breakdowns and improving vehicle lifespan.

- **Business Outcome**: Reduced maintenance costs and increased vehicle uptime.

- **Sample KPI**: 20% reduction in maintenance costs, 15% increase in vehicle lifespan.

74. AI-POWERED PERSONALIZED MARKETING CAMPAIGNS

- **Description**: AI creates customized marketing campaigns based on customer preferences and past behavior.

- **Business Outcome**: Higher customer engagement and conversion rates.

- **Sample KPI**: 30% increase in campaign effectiveness, 25% improvement in customer engagement.

75. AI-DRIVEN FINANCIAL PORTFOLIO OPTIMIZATION

- **Description**: AI helps financial advisors optimize investment portfolios by predicting market trends and risk.

- **Business Outcome**: Improved investment returns and better risk management.

- **Sample KPI**: 10% increase in portfolio returns, 20% reduction in portfolio risk.

76. AI FOR REAL-TIME LANGUAGE TRANSLATION

- **Description**: AI offers real-time translation of languages to facilitate communication between people speaking different languages.
- **Business Outcome**: Enhanced global collaboration and improved customer support.
- **Sample KPI**: 20% increase in global customer satisfaction, 30% faster resolution of multilingual support queries.

77. AI-POWERED PERSONALIZED SHOPPING EXPERIENCE

- **Description**: AI uses customer preferences, browsing history, and purchase behavior to create a personalized online shopping experience.

- **Business Outcome**: Increased conversion rates and enhanced customer loyalty.

- **Sample KPI**: 20% increase in online sales, 25% improvement in customer loyalty metrics.

78. AI FOR AUTONOMOUS DELIVERY VEHICLES

- **Description**: AI powers autonomous delivery systems to transport goods efficiently without human drivers.

- **Business Outcome**: Reduced delivery costs and faster delivery times.

- **Sample KPI**: 30% reduction in delivery costs, 20% increase in delivery speed.

79. AI-ENHANCED LEARNING MANAGEMENT SYSTEMS

- **Description**: AI tailors training programs to the needs and skills of individual employees.
- **Business Outcome**: Improved employee learning outcomes and skill development.
- **Sample KPI**: 25% increase in employee learning outcomes, 20% improvement in training engagement.

80. AI-POWERED PREDICTIVE SALES LEAD SCORING

- **Description**: AI predicts the likelihood of sales leads converting into customers by analyzing historical data.

- **Business Outcome**: Increased sales efficiency and higher conversion rates.

- **Sample KPI**: 15% increase in lead conversion rates, 10% improvement in sales productivity.

81. AI FOR SUPPLY CHAIN OPTIMIZATION

- **Description**: AI optimizes supply chain operations by predicting demand, managing inventory, and identifying inefficiencies.

- **Business Outcome**: Reduced operational costs and improved supply chain resilience.

- **Sample KPI**: 10% reduction in inventory costs, 15% improvement in on-time delivery performance.

82. AI-POWERED VIRTUAL REALITY EXPERIENCES

- **Description**: AI enhances virtual reality experiences by dynamically adjusting environments based on user interactions.

- **Business Outcome**: Immersive experiences for training, marketing, and entertainment.

- **Sample KPI**: 25% increase in user engagement, 20% improvement in training effectiveness.

83. AI FOR DYNAMIC WORKLOAD MANAGEMENT

- **Description**: AI optimizes the allocation of tasks and resources based on workload demand and team capacity.

- **Business Outcome**: Improved workforce efficiency and resource utilization.

- **Sample KPI**: 20% improvement in team productivity, 10% reduction in project delays.

84. AI FOR AUTOMATED COMPLIANCE MONITORING

- **Description**: AI monitors business processes and transactions to ensure compliance with industry regulations and standards.

- **Business Outcome**: Reduced compliance risk and operational overhead.

- **Sample KPI**: 30% reduction in compliance violations, 15% improvement in compliance reporting accuracy.

85. AI FOR PREDICTING EMPLOYEE TURNOVER

- **Description**: AI predicts which employees are at risk of leaving the company based on various factors like job satisfaction and performance.

- **Business Outcome**: Reduced employee turnover and improved talent retention.

- **Sample KPI**: 15% reduction in employee turnover, 10% improvement in employee satisfaction.

86. AI-POWERED INFLUENCER MARKETING

- **Description**: AI analyzes social media data to identify key influencers and predict the effectiveness of influencer marketing campaigns.

- **Business Outcome**: Improved marketing ROI and enhanced brand visibility.

- **Sample KPI**: 25% increase in ROI from influencer campaigns, 20% increase in brand awareness.

87. AI FOR VOICE-ACTIVATED CUSTOMER SUPPORT

- **Description**: AI enables customers to interact with support systems using voice commands, improving ease of use.
- **Business Outcome**: Enhanced customer support experience and reduced response time.
- **Sample KPI**: 20% reduction in response time, 15% increase in customer satisfaction.

88. AI FOR FINANCIAL FORECASTING

- **Description**: AI analyzes financial data and market trends to generate more accurate financial forecasts.

- **Business Outcome**: Better budgeting and financial planning.

- **Sample KPI**: 20% improvement in forecasting accuracy, 10% reduction in financial forecasting errors.

89. AI FOR AUTOMATED NEWS GENERATION

- **Description**: AI automatically generates news stories based on available data, ensuring timely and accurate reporting.

- **Business Outcome**: Faster content production and improved journalism efficiency.

- **Sample KPI**: 30% reduction in content production time, 25% increase in reader engagement.

90. AI-POWERED SPORTS PERFORMANCE ANALYTICS

- **Description**: AI analyzes athletes' performance data to provide insights into strengths, weaknesses, and potential for improvement.
- **Business Outcome**: Improved athletic performance and more effective training programs.
- **Sample KPI**: 20% improvement in athlete performance, 15% reduction in injury rates.

91. AI FOR CUSTOMER BEHAVIOR PREDICTION

- **Description**: AI predicts future customer actions, helping businesses anticipate needs and personalize offers.
- **Business Outcome**: More effective marketing and higher conversion rates.
- **Sample KPI**: 20% increase in conversions, 15% increase in customer engagement.

92. AI FOR FRAUD DETECTION IN BANKING

- **Description**: AI identifies unusual banking transactions, preventing fraud in real-time.
- **Business Outcome**: Enhanced fraud prevention and improved security.
- **Sample KPI**: 25% reduction in fraudulent transactions, 20% improvement in fraud detection accuracy.

93. AI-DRIVEN CONTENT MODERATION

- **Description**: AI automates the process of detecting and moderating inappropriate or harmful content online.

- **Business Outcome**: Enhanced platform safety and improved user experience.

- **Sample KPI**: 40% reduction in harmful content, 30% faster moderation times.

94. AI FOR AUTOMATED RECRUITING AND TALENT SOURCING

- **Description**: AI automates candidate sourcing, screening, and matching for open job positions.

- **Business Outcome**: Reduced time-to-hire and improved candidate quality.

- **Sample KPI**: 25% reduction in hiring time, 15% improvement in candidate quality.

95. AI-POWERED TRAVEL PLANNING ASSISTANCE

- **Description**: AI helps travelers plan trips by analyzing preferences, budgets, and previous trips to suggest itineraries.
- **Business Outcome**: Enhanced customer satisfaction and increased travel bookings.
- **Sample KPI**: 20% increase in travel bookings, 15% improvement in customer satisfaction.

96. AI FOR SMART HOME AUTOMATION

- **Description**: AI powers smart homes by adjusting lighting, temperature, and security systems based on user preferences and behaviors.

- **Business Outcome**: Improved energy efficiency and user comfort.

- **Sample KPI**: 15% reduction in energy consumption, 20% increase in user comfort.

97. AI FOR AUTOMATED SUPPLY CHAIN RISK MANAGEMENT

- **Description**: AI identifies risks in the supply chain, such as potential disruptions or delays, and recommends mitigations.

- **Business Outcome**: Reduced supply chain disruptions and improved operational efficiency.

- **Sample KPI**: 20% reduction in supply chain disruptions, 15% improvement in risk mitigation response times.

98. AI FOR CONTENT A/B TESTING

- **Description**: AI automates A/B testing of digital content to identify which versions drive higher engagement.

- **Business Outcome**: Increased content engagement and more effective marketing strategies.

- **Sample KPI**: 20% increase in content engagement, 10% improvement in conversion rates.

99. AI-POWERED CUSTOMER RETARGETING

- **Description**: AI uses customer data to retarget visitors with personalized ads based on their browsing behavior and past interactions.

- **Business Outcome**: Higher conversion rates and increased ROI on advertising spend.

- **Sample KPI**: 25% increase in conversion rates, 15% improvement in ad spend ROI.

100. AI-ENHANCED SENTIMENT ANALYSIS FOR EMPLOYEE FEEDBACK

- **Description**: AI analyzes employee feedback to gauge sentiment and identify areas for improvement.
- **Business Outcome**: Improved employee satisfaction and organizational culture.
- **Sample KPI**: 20% improvement in employee satisfaction, 15% reduction in turnover rates.

END NOTES: HOW TO USE THESE USE CASES TO BRING VALUE TO YOUR CLIENTS

As you've explored the top 100 AI use cases throughout this book, it's clear that AI offers transformative potential across a vast array of industries and business functions. By leveraging the knowledge and insights from these use cases, you can drive tangible value for your clients in several key ways.

1. UNDERSTAND CLIENT NEEDS AND CONTEXT

The first step in applying these use cases is to deeply understand the unique challenges and objectives your client faces. Every organization operates in a different context—whether it's dealing with customer service, optimizing operations, enhancing product development, or improving security. Once you have a clear understanding of their pain points and goals, you can identify the AI use cases that align best with their needs.

For instance, a client in retail may benefit from AI-driven product recommendation engines or customer segmentation, while a financial institution might find value in AI-powered fraud detection and predictive analytics.

2. TAILOR SOLUTIONS TO SPECIFIC BUSINESS OUTCOMES

Not all use cases will apply directly in their off-the-shelf form. It's important to adapt the use case to meet the specific objectives your client is trying to achieve. For example, an AI-powered customer support chatbot may need to be customized to address particular industry requirements, language nuances, or integration with existing systems to deliver the desired business outcomes.

Focus on delivering measurable results, such as improved customer satisfaction, reduced operational costs, or increased revenue. Make sure the AI solution you propose aligns with the business's strategic vision and is framed in terms of business value (e.g., enhanced user experience, better decision-making, cost reduction).

3. DEMONSTRATE THE ROI OF AI

Clients often seek tangible proof that AI investments will drive value. Using the KPIs associated with each use case, you can show clients the expected return on investment (ROI). By demonstrating clear performance metrics—such as reduced time to market, increased conversion rates, or cost savings—you can highlight how AI can transform their business.

For example, in the case of AI for predictive maintenance in manufacturing, you could show how it would lead to a reduction in downtime by 30% and a 15% decrease in maintenance costs, helping the client understand the direct impact on their bottom line.

4. FOSTER A DATA-DRIVEN CULTURE

The success of AI implementation depends on the quality and accessibility of data. Encourage your clients to adopt a data-driven mindset that prioritizes the collection, organization, and analysis of data. Help them understand how data from across their organization—whether it's sales, customer behavior, operational logs, or market trends—can be used to build AI models that improve decision-making and drive innovation.

As you work through the use cases, guide them in how to enhance their data infrastructure, ensuring that the data is clean, accessible, and actionable.

5. FOCUS ON CONTINUOUS IMPROVEMENT

AI adoption is not a one-time project but a continuous journey. As clients implement AI solutions, encourage them to view the initial deployment as just the beginning. Leverage AI to monitor system performance, track KPIs, and iterate on solutions. This continuous feedback loop allows AI to become smarter over time, improving both the systems and the outcomes.

For example, after deploying AI-driven chatbots for customer support, regularly monitor metrics like response time, resolution rate, and customer satisfaction. Based on these insights, refine the bot's algorithms and expand its scope to handle more complex queries.

6. ADDRESS ETHICAL AI AND GOVERNANCE

With the increased adoption of AI comes responsibility. As an AI consultant or practitioner, it's vital to ensure that AI systems are built, deployed, and monitored with fairness, transparency, and ethical considerations in mind. This includes ensuring data privacy, mitigating biases in AI algorithms, and complying with relevant regulations.

Help your clients understand the importance of AI governance frameworks and best practices that can help mitigate potential risks and safeguard against unintended consequences. Establishing clear ethical guidelines in their AI initiatives is critical to building trust and securing long-term success.

7. FOSTER COLLABORATION BETWEEN AI AND HUMAN TEAMS

AI excels in automating repetitive tasks, generating insights from vast datasets, and making data-driven predictions, but human expertise remains crucial for strategic decision-making, creative tasks, and complex problem-solving.

Encourage your clients to integrate AI in a way that complements and empowers their teams. For example, AI-powered tools can help human teams by providing insights, automating mundane tasks, and enhancing decision-making processes, but human oversight and interpretation are still necessary for making final decisions.

8. BUILD A SCALABLE AI ECOSYSTEM

As your clients begin to realize the benefits of AI in one area of their business, they will likely want to expand the use of AI to other domains. Help them build a scalable AI ecosystem that allows them to easily implement additional AI use cases across departments and functions. This includes setting up the right AI infrastructure, training staff, and establishing processes for rolling out new AI initiatives effectively.

For example, if your client successfully implements AI-driven sales forecasting, they might want to extend AI usage to areas like inventory optimization, marketing campaign management, and customer experience enhancement.

9. EMPOWER CLIENTS TO BECOME AI CHAMPIONS

Ultimately, the goal is to not only implement AI solutions but also to empower your clients to become champions of AI within their organization. Provide them with the tools, knowledge, and training they need to take ownership of their AI projects and drive innovation forward.

Offer guidance on building an AI strategy, cultivating a culture of innovation, and continuously exploring new ways to leverage AI for competitive advantage. Equip your clients with the understanding that AI is not just a technology—it's a business enabler that will shape the future of their industry.

CONCLUSION

By leveraging these 100 AI use cases, you now have a comprehensive toolkit to help clients identify and implement AI solutions that can revolutionize their business. Whether they are just starting their AI journey or are looking to expand their AI capabilities, these use cases provide the insights and strategies needed to deliver real, measurable business outcomes.

Your role as an AI consultant or practitioner is to help your clients navigate this journey with expertise, strategy, and a clear focus on achieving value. By applying the knowledge and practices in this book, you can guide them to embrace AI and become true champions of the technology, driving success in the digital age.

Now, armed with these use cases and best practices, it's time for you to go forth and help your clients unlock the full potential of AI. Let their transformation begin.

www.ingramcontent.com/pod-product-compliance
Lightning Source LLC
LaVergne TN
LVHW041210050326
832903LV00021B/565